PUFFIN BOOKS

MAKE SOME NOISE

MAKE SOME NOISE

THE HORNE SECTION

ILLUSTRATED BY ROB FLOWERS

PUFFIN

Please supervise children during the activities and tasks described in this book, use appropriate safety measures at all times and follow the health and safety advice provided. The activities described are undertaken at the participants' own risk and the author and publishers disclaim, as far as the law allows, any liability arising directly or indirectly from the use or misuse of any information contained in this book.

The material in this book is intended to be humorous. In some cases true life figures are mentioned and some references and descriptions of events are substantially fictitious and the products of the authors' imagination.

This book goes out to all you people out there who have ever eaten breakfast.

PUFFIN BOOKS

UK | USA | Canada | Ireland | Australia
India | New Zealand | South Africa

Puffin Books are part of the Penguin Random House group of companies whose addresses can be found at global.penguinrandomhouse.com.
www.penguin.co.uk   www.puffin.co.uk   www.ladybird.co.uk

Penguin Random House UK

First published 2024

001

Text copyright © Shakey Productions, 2024
Illustration copyright © Rob Flowers 2024

The moral right of the authors, illustrator and copyright holders has been asserted

Printed and bound in Great Britain by Clays Ltd, Elcograf S.p.A.

The authorized representative in the EEA is Penguin Random House Ireland, Morrison Chambers, 32 Nassau Street, Dublin, D02 YH68

A CIP catalogue record for this book is available from the British Library

ISBN: 978–0–241–64972–5

All correspondence to:
Puffin Books
Penguin Random House Children's UK
One Embassy Gardens, 8 Viaduct Gardens
London SW11 7BW

Penguin Random House is committed to a sustainable future for our business, our readers and our planet. This book is made from Forest Stewardship Council® certified paper.

CONTENTS

1. WHAT IS THE POINT OF THIS BOOK? — 1
2. WHAT DO I NEED TO MAKE MUSIC? — 31
3. WHAT DO ALL THE DOTS AND SQUIGGLES MEAN? — 77
4. WHAT SORT OF MUSIC SHOULD I MAKE? — 103
5. WHERE SHOULD I PLAY MY MUSIC? — 153
6. HOW WILL PEOPLE HEAR MY MUSIC? — 175
7. THE MUSIC RECORD BREAKERS — 211
8. CAN WE WRITE A SONG NOW? — 235
9. WHAT WAS ALL THAT ABOUT? — 263

MORE SONGS AND LYRICS — 275

GLOSSARY — 282

CHAPTER

ONE

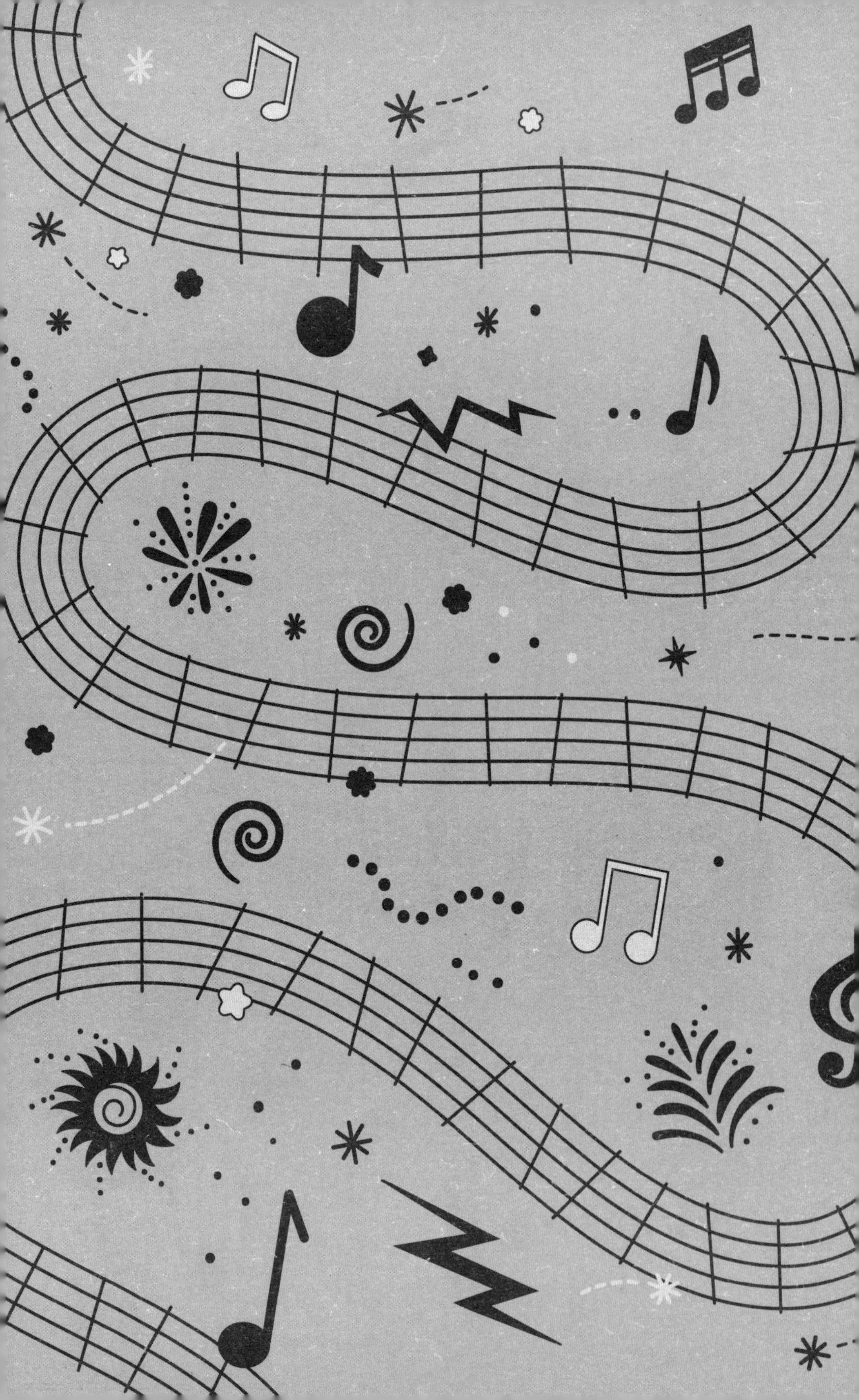

WHAT IS THE POINT OF THIS BOOK?

Music is everywhere. You can probably hear it right now. Shut your eyes. There: hear the rumble of your neighbour's rubbish car, the clanging of someone walking too close to a radiator, the distant barking of a dog and the desperate whistling of its owner. Can you hear someone blowing bubbles in their drink through a straw or a gust of wind knocking down your dustbin?

That's music! Or, at least, that's sound. And so it might become music. Because sound is the basis of all music.

(ALSO, I DIDN'T SAY OPEN YOUR EYES AGAIN. IF YOU'RE READING THIS, YOU'RE CHEATING.)

OK, you can open them now.

You can choose not to go fishing and refuse to eat broccoli, but you can't avoid music. You can't put your fingers in your ears all the time and block out all the noise and sound around you, because eventually you're going to need to do other things like tying your shoelaces and dipping your chips in ketchup.

Music is all around you, and chances are you're going to listen to over a million songs in your lifetime...

EVERY YEAR YOU'LL HEAR MUSIC FOR MORE THAN 730 HOURS. THAT'S THIRTY DAYS OF SOLID TUNES THAT STARTED IN SOMEONE ELSE'S HEAD AND ENDED UP IN YOURS.

In a single day you'll hear about two hours of music. That's about fifty songs. **EVERY DAY!** Can you name fifty songs? I can, but only after thinking about it really hard for a week, in which time I'll have heard another 350.

No matter who you are, music is going to play a big part in your life. Everywhere you go, music will go too.

95% of the world's population listen to a song by British singer and songwriter Ed Sheeran at least once every day and twice at the weekend.

BUT WHO ARE WE AND WHAT IS THE ACTUAL POINT OF THIS BOOK?

My name is Alex Horne, and I'm in charge of a comedy jazz band called the Horne Section. They're here with me too but I'm writing this bit because they're all holding their instruments.

We love playing music, and we love making people laugh. And as a comedy band we sometimes even make people laugh while we play them music. We perform what we think are funny songs up and down the country, appearing on radio and TV. We even have our own TV show. We play jazz music, but also things like pop and rock and country. (We'll talk about all the different types of music in Chapter 4.) While we like to mess around, some of us do actually know quite a bit about music, so we've decided to share everything we know with you. And because making music is one of the most fun things there is, we want to help you make your own music too.

> Hi there, I'm Ed and I play the piano. Alex was lying before when he said we were all holding our instruments. I wasn't carrying my piano. I can carry my piano because I'm very strong, but I wasn't then. Anyway, I just wanted to pop up to say hello ... Hello.

That's one of the musicians. And that's the sort of thing they do. You'll see them popping up a lot throughout this book with some annoying (and *sometimes* useful) things to say. They are more talented than me, though, so I keep them around to make music.

With this book as your handy guide, you and your friends could start a band just like us. Because if you're going to start a band, you need to know a lot of important musical information. Not the boring rubbish you learn at school, though – this is the funny, gross and mind-blowing stuff. This book is packed with bizarre tales, unbelievable musical history and bonkers facts about instruments (including one that's bigger than a cricket pitch). We'll also tell you about what types of music there are, what all the different instruments look and sound like, and how you can become a musician without spending thirty years in a room all by yourself learning scales (like one of our band members did).

> Yes, I have spent a long time in one room playing the same notes over and over again, but I don't have any regrets. I had a nice view of the park and I got to eat crisps all day.

From picking your band mates, finding the best instrument for you, discovering the music you want to play (and much more), we're going to take you on a rip-roaring journey through sound as you find your way to musical legend status. But before we go further, let's start with the most important lesson of all, which is this: absolutely anyone can start playing music. Anyone! I am not a musician. I am a comedian. I didn't study music at school or university.

So while I can make people laugh I'm no expert in all the technical musical stuff. But because I'm very funny (and my name sounds like a musical instrument) I have found my place in the Horne Section doing the important stuff like waving a stick around and being really enthusiastic.

Whether you play no instruments, one instrument or many instruments, whether you come from a family of musicians or you've never even seen a piano before, I promise that you ARE a musician. You live and breathe music, just like the rest of us, possibly without even realizing. So warm up those vocal cords and prepare to laugh and learn a lot, as we dive into the amazing story of sound.

THE BAND

So let me introduce you to the silly people in my band who have written this book with me. (It's worth noting that each one of them looks a little bit like the instrument they play.)

JOE AUCKLAND
THE TRUMPETER

LOOKS LIKE AN OVERGROWN SCRUFFY BABY, BUT PLAYS TRUMPET LIKE AN ANGEL

- Powerful lips
- Also plays the banjo and wears funny silver rings
- Furry head like a kiwi (fruit or bird)
- Chops his food with a fork and scoops it up with his knife
- Able to fall asleep within three minutes because he is more like a dog than a human

MARK BROWN
THE SAXOPHONIST

GRUMPY POP LEGEND

- Very long tongue and powerful jaw – as every saxophone player needs
- Never been late
- Never been ill
- Wrote his own facts about himself because he always thinks he'll do a better job than anyone else

WILLIP COLLIER
THE BASSIST

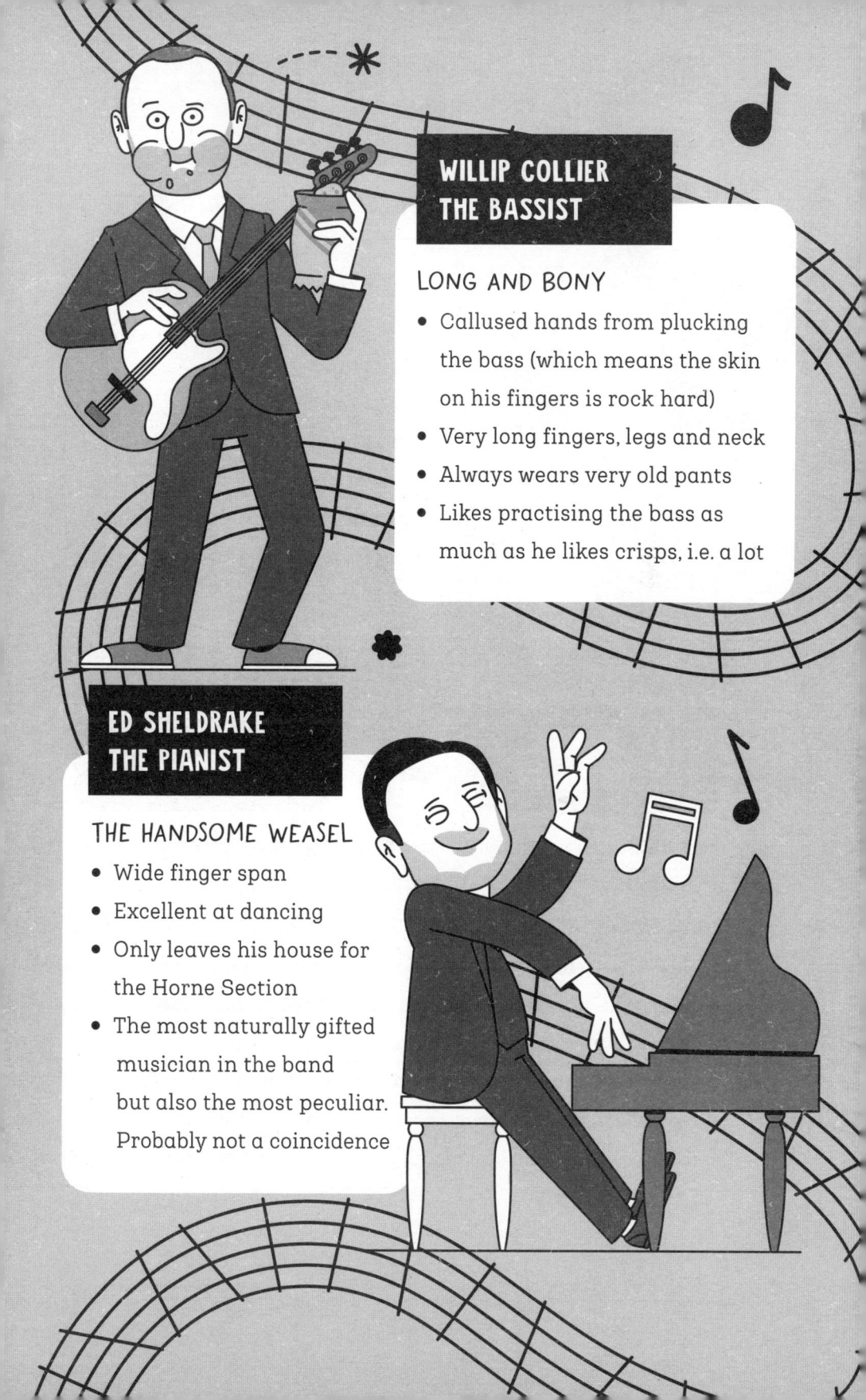

LONG AND BONY

- Callused hands from plucking the bass (which means the skin on his fingers is rock hard)
- Very long fingers, legs and neck
- Always wears very old pants
- Likes practising the bass as much as he likes crisps, i.e. a lot

ED SHELDRAKE
THE PIANIST

THE HANDSOME WEASEL

- Wide finger span
- Excellent at dancing
- Only leaves his house for the Horne Section
- The most naturally gifted musician in the band but also the most peculiar. Probably not a coincidence

BEN REYNOLDS THE DRUMMER

HAPPIEST WHEN HE'S HITTING HIS NOISY CIRCLES (OR, AS HE CALLS THEM, CYMBALS AND DRUMS) AGAIN AND AGAIN

- Two hands, two feet
- Muscles, big muscles
- Can't burp
- Scared of eggs
- A smiley boy who can't believe he gets to make a living playing drums

ALEX HORNE THE CONDUCTOR

AND THIS IS ME. I TELL EVERYONE WHAT MUSIC TO PLAY AND HOW FAST TO PLAY IT (THERE'S A LITTLE BIT MORE TO CONDUCTING BUT MORE ON THAT LATER).

- Has a lectern and a baton (a stand and a stick)
- Thinks he's in charge of the band but can't read music
- Zero talent, maximum enthusiasm
- Has a bad habit of making up facts for fun
- One of the few people in the world to have an extra (hidden) ear, so he can usually hear music coming before anyone else

As you can see, I am the most important member of the band. By miles. But throughout this book I'm going to have chats with my band members, who can offer some true tales and fascinating facts about music.

For our first band chat let's see if we can find out what music actually is. Because despite what I said at the start, it's not quite as simple as a bin falling over while a dog barks...

> I don't actually know how to conduct or play any music, but I *think* I do, and that's what counts.

BAND CHAT

Alex: So what is music?

Band: Great question, Alex.

Alex: It's Alex Horne.

Band: Great question, Alex Horne. Well, music is a collection of different sounds that have been organized in such a way that they make you want to dance, smile, cry or buy things after watching an advert.

Band: To get a bit more technical, music is generally thought to consist of four things:

1 MELODY
A series of sounds organized into a tune.

2 HARMONY
A collection of musical notes that sound good when played together.

3 RHYTHM
A strong pattern of words, sounds or notes.

4 TONE
The qualities of the actual sound of the notes and what makes one note sound different from another. If you want to talk about the tone of a song, use words like 'brassy', 'bright' or 'reedy' ('reedy' refers to the reed that all woodwind instruments have and isn't anything to do with books).

Band: As you can probably tell from our clumsy descriptions, all these things are easier to hear than describe. So how about you turn on the radio or the TV? If you don't have a radio because you're not as old as us, or you're reading this somewhere with no TV, like your bedroom or a submarine, here are some examples:

Imagine someone's having a bowl of cereal. They clink their spoon on the bowl slowly at first before speeding up. That pattern of sounds is the **RHYTHM**.

Now imagine it's your birthday. All your friends are at your house and your mum has called you in from the garden. She turns the lights out, brings out a cake and she alone sings 'Happy Birthday'. Then your friends join in with the **MELODY** to create sweet, sweet music. Their voices together create a **HARMONY**.

Or imagine you are watching your dog in the garden. She has taken a flipflop from the house and is holding it in her mouth and shaking it as hard as she can. The flipflop splits, falls to the ground and she stares at it. Then she barks at it. Once, twice, three times. And then she does a wee nearby. Did you notice the different **TONES** in all those sounds? No? Well, you're right, that wasn't music. That was just a dog shouting at a flipflop.

Alex: Thanks, band, that was a great answer. But also it was quite a boring answer, and this is meant to be a funny book. So please could you try again but make it more fun? This time you've got to answer the question 'What is music?' in under sixty-five words and the last one has to be 'food'.

Band: Music is a mixture of lovely, beautiful or sometimes even scary sounds made by musical instruments creating **VIBRATIONS** in the air. These vibrations make their way into your ears and along to your brain. Imagine the most delicious and horrible meals you've ever tasted, and all the meals in between, and you have to eat these meals with your ears. Music is ear food.

Alex: Well, there we go. Music is like baked beans. We all know what baked beans do; they taste great and help us make wonderful funny sounds. That's music! And why is there so much music around?

Band: Because it makes us feel good. It makes us happier and healthier. In a way music is like medicine. Listening to music has been found to make us feel less worried. Depending on what music you listen to, it can also help you sleep, be more alert or remember things better. It improves our mood and helps us communicate with the people around us. It makes us excited and then calms us down. Music can really change an experience or situation, whether you're watching football, eating in a restaurant, having a birthday party, watching a movie or trying to build the highest tower of potatoes on a plate in a bouncy castle. And scientists have also found that listening to music releases **DOPAMINE** and **ENDORPHINS**.

Alex: I don't know what dopamine and endorphins are. They sound like they live in the sea.

Band: They don't live in the sea, Alex. Dopamine and endorphins are chemicals made by your body, and when they are released in your brain they make you feel good. Things like exercise and music can release dopamine and boost your happiness!

ALEX HAS LEFT THE CONVERSATION.

BUT WHAT *ACTUALLY* IS MUSIC?

So far we've said that music is a lot of different things, but if you go into a music class with a bowl of baked beans and say you're ready for your lesson, your teacher might not be too impressed. The trouble is, while my band really do know their stuff, they're also very silly and find farting funny. So let's check what some of the world's great and serious musicians, writers and artists believe music is:

> Music is what feelings sound like.

Aldous Huxley (1894–1963), writer.

Music doesn't lie.

Jimi Hendrix (1942-1970), guitarist, singer, songwriter.

Are you sure it doesn't lie? The Beatles had a song called 'I Am the Walrus' and none of them had tusks. Jimi Hendrix himself sang 'I was the first man on the moon' and that's definitely not true. Shakira said her hips don't lie, but that's another matter.

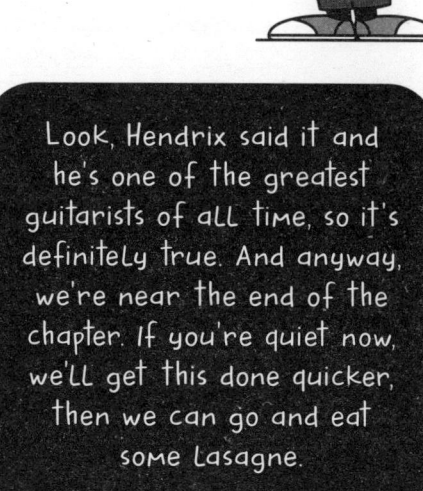

Look, Hendrix said it and he's one of the greatest guitarists of all time, so it's definitely true. And anyway, we're near the end of the chapter. If you're quiet now, we'll get this done quicker, then we can go and eat some lasagne.

19

> ## Music is the universal language of mankind.

Henry Wadsworth Longfellow (1807–1882), poet.

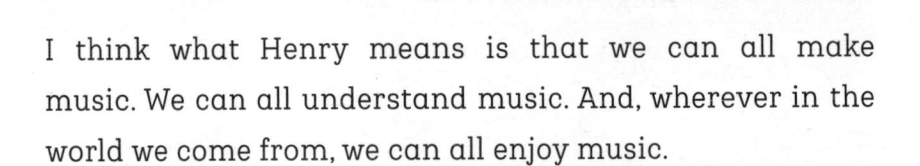

I think what Henry means is that we can all make music. We can all understand music. And, wherever in the world we come from, we can all enjoy music.

BUT THAT STILL DOESN'T ANSWER THE QUESTION OF WHAT MUSIC ACTUALLY IS!

Why don't we ask the dictionary?
It defines music as:

> ## sounds combined in such a way as to produce beauty of form, harmony and expression of emotion.

I don't think that really helps us either. But I feel like I've learned enough to have a go at writing my own definition...

> **Music is nice-sounding noise made by people.**
>
> **Alex Horne (1978–now), former child, current writer, leader of the Horne Section.**

That will have to do for now.

IMPRESS YOUR FRIENDS AND FAMILY WITH YOUR INCREDIBLE KNOWLEDGE

Before I hand over to the band, who are going to take you on your musical journey, I should say that in order to make sure this book isn't too boring, I'll also be chipping in with comments, musical interludes, unbelievable stories and general nonsense.

I'm going to tell you lots of musical facts, but I'll also be telling you a lot of lies. I'll come clean and tell you which ones you shouldn't have believed at the end of each chapter. It will keep you on your toes, so you'll need to have your eyes peeled and your ears pricked. (I have already told two lies by the way.)

Here are a few facts to get you started:

1 Plants grow faster when there's music playing nearby. Some serious scientists (who were meant to be studying something called agricultural biotechnology in South Korea) played fourteen different classical pieces of music in some fields where rice was growing. There were some other fields where rice was growing, where they *didn't* play any music. And they discovered that the rice grew quicker in the fields where they played music! Their conclusion? Crops can actually 'hear', and ARE ALWAYS LISTENING. So you should only tell secrets in multistorey car parks and swimming pools.

2 Cows produce more milk when listening to music, but that music has to be slow and calm. It goes back to the dopamine and endorphins we talked about earlier. Relaxing music relieves stress, even for cows. Being milked must be fairly stressful, but the right sort of music can help with that.

> We know that cows and plants listen to music, but I do want to make it clear that they're not very good at making it. Daffodils can't press down the keys on a piano and bulls can't get a decent grip on a flute. So if you're buying concert tickets, I'd recommend going to see human musicians like us.

> Good point, Ed. Although birds actually love making music and do it all the time. Scientists have even found that their brains react to music in the same way ours do. They sing to communicate with other birds and attract mates. Parrots also dance for the same reason! I'm genuinely worried that one day I'll be replaced by a thrush.

3 In a survey carried out by youthmusic.org.uk, 97% of young people listened to music in the last week, 85% of young singers say singing makes them happy and 30% of young people play a musical instrument. A different study showed that 95% of Australian kids listen to serious jazz music. (This is great news for us because we, the Horne Section, are one of the top one hundred comedy jazz bands in Europe.)

MUSICAL TASKS

As well as being the leader of my band I also make a TV show called *Taskmaster*, on which comedians compete to do silly challenges. It's been around for a while now and lots of kids watch it, even though sometimes the grown-ups use words other grown-ups think they shouldn't be using.

In the show I invent lots of the tasks and then act as a referee while they're being carried out. So while I'm here (and because I'm not actually very good at music myself), I thought I could set you some musical tasks. That way I'm still definitely a very important person in the band.

The tasks will be at the end of each chapter – find a friend or sibling to compete against, and ask someone you trust to decide on the winner. Here is your first one:

MUSICAL TASK NUMBER ONE

For one whole day you must shout the word 'MUSIC' every time you hear a piece of music.

If you fail to shout the word 'MUSIC' when you hear a piece of music, you must start again the following day.

Most consecutive, successful 'MUSIC' days wins.

YOUR TIME STARTS NOW.

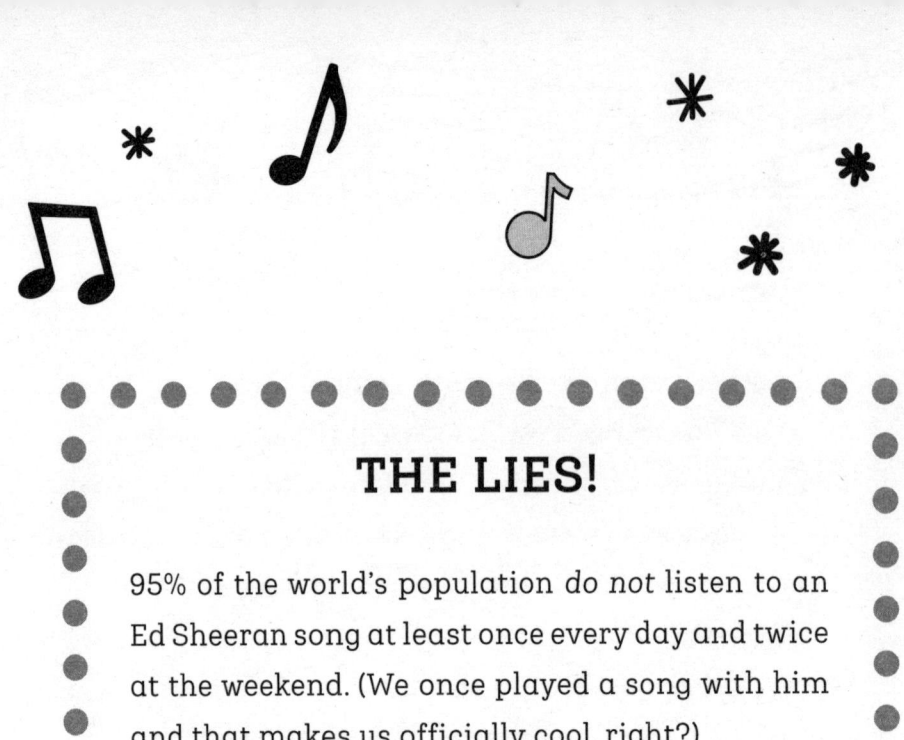

THE LIES!

95% of the world's population *do not* listen to an Ed Sheeran song at least once every day and twice at the weekend. (We once played a song with him and that makes us officially cool, right?)

95% of Australian kids *don't* listen to serious jazz music. Disappointingly jazz is officially the least popular category of music in the world! So despite being officially cool, we are also officially unpopular. It is always cool to be different, though, so give it a go!

And finally I don't have an extra hidden ear. I wish I did, though.

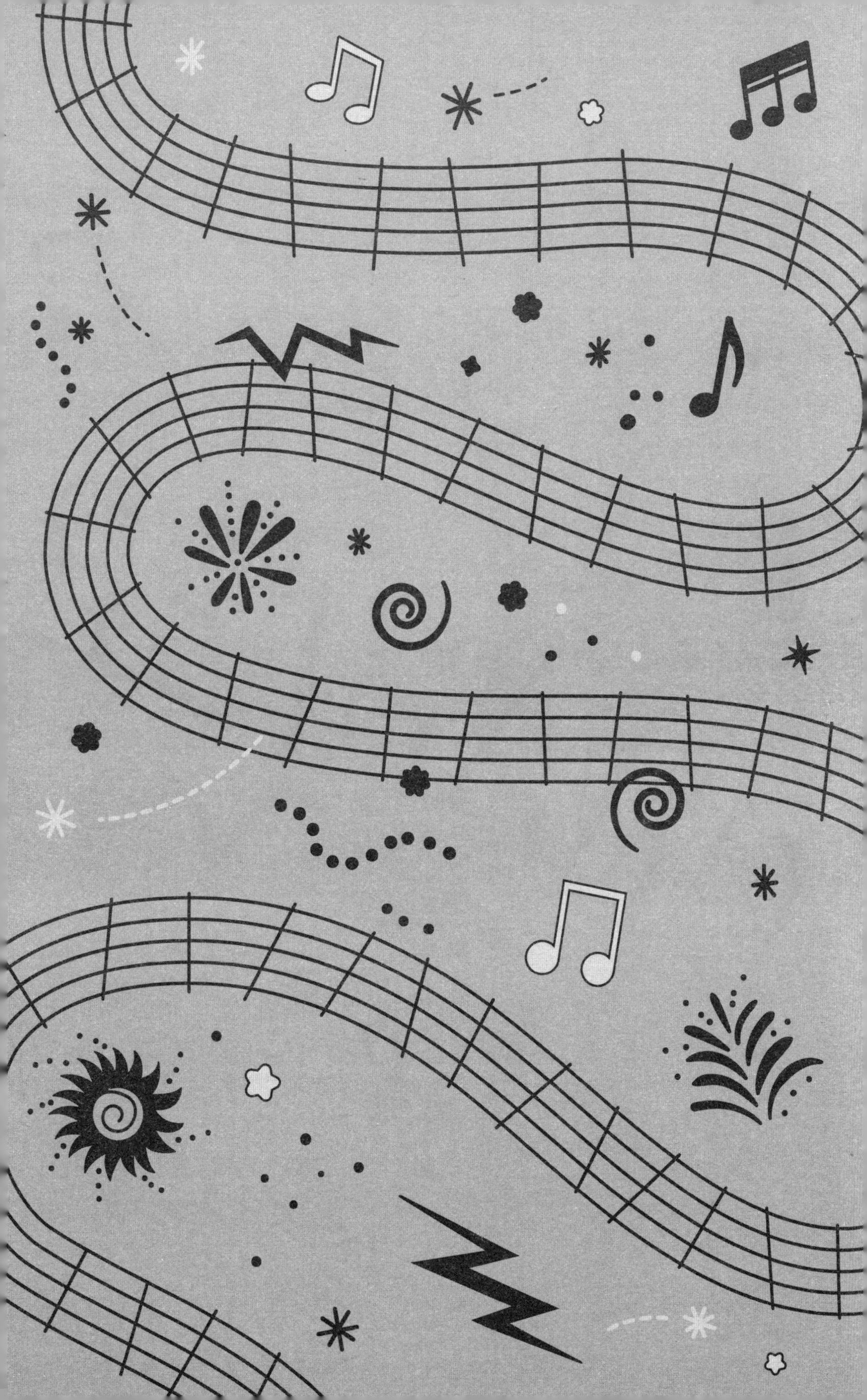

CHAPTER

TWO

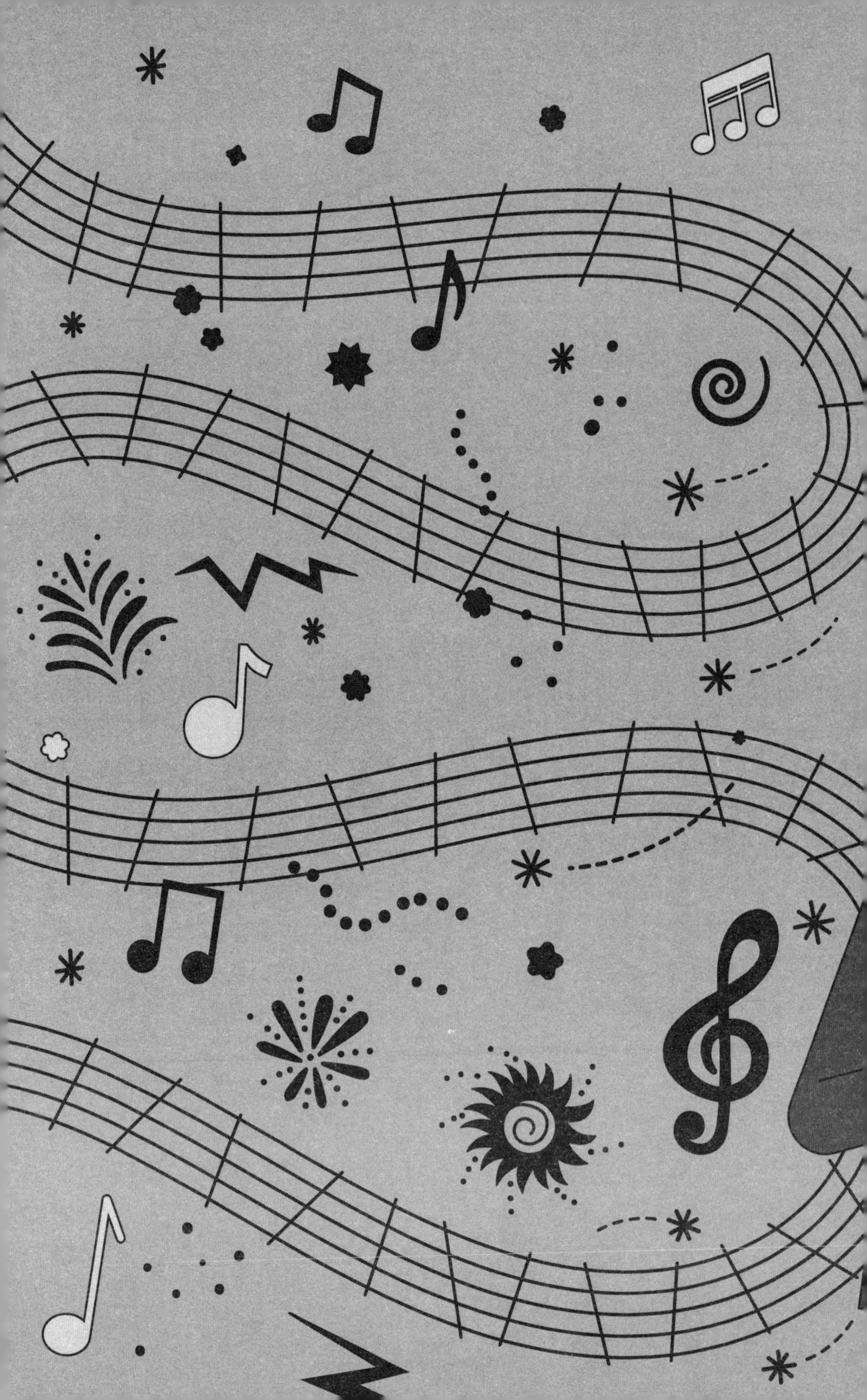

WHAT DO I NEED TO MAKE MUSIC?

As the front man of our band, the conductor and the most important person, I don't actually play trumpet or drums or guitar or anything really. But I do know that instruments are definitely one of the main things you need to make music. Instead of learning to play these things, I decided to find people who can play them for me. I'm now going to let those people tell you all about the many different kinds of instruments out there so you can either choose one yourself or, like me, persuade a friend to do so.

BAND CHAT

Alex: OK then, band, please tell our readers about all the musical instruments. Remember to try to be interesting at all times.

Band: Yes, sir!

Alex: Go on then...

Band: We're ready.

Alex: Great... So, band, what do I need to make music?

Band: The instruments!

Alex: Yes, I said that in my excellent introduction.

Band: Mmm, we read that. We don't think you are the most important person in the band...

Alex: Shhh. Please can you just tell us about the instruments? Also, please can you make it fun? Maybe start with four facts and one joke.

Band: Fine. Here goes:

1. There are over 1,500 musical instruments.

2. The pop star Prince played twenty-seven of them on his debut **ALBUM**, For You.

3. Alex Horne cannot play a single one! That's zero out of 1,500!

4. The oldest musical instrument is a 60,000-year-old flute. That's amazing and I'll give you the bare bones of the story now.

The flute was made from bear bones.

Alex: If the jokes don't get any better, I'm going to put jelly in your trumpet, sausages in your saxophone and Marmite on your drumsticks.

ALEX HAS LEFT THE CONVERSATION.

SURFING THE SOUND WAVES

Before we meet the different instruments, it's important to understand how we actually hear the noises they all make. As you might have guessed, ears have quite a large role to play in the hearing of noises. People don't talk a lot about ears. It's rare you hear someone being praised for having particularly skilful or brilliant ears. You can't see your own ones without a mirror and very few people can wiggle them.

When was the last time you showed some appreciation for your ears? Go to the bathroom right now and have a good look at yours. Or maybe go and have a very close look at someone else's. Peek right inside. Horrible, aren't they?

But they do a very good job at trapping the invisible noises that come their way. All the folds and flaps help **AMPLIFY** the sounds, funnelling them into a bit called the ear canal, where they smash into your eardrums. If we didn't have ears, music might well not exist.

Sounds are made up of waves, which are formed by tiny little objects (called **MOLECULES**) vibrating. When a sound is made, our ears trap these sound waves, sort of in the same way that your hands might catch a ball.

Let's make some sound waves now. Clap your hands!

Have you done it? Great. By bashing your hands together you've just made a load of tiny molecules move around in the shape of a wave, and the noise you heard was the sound wave reaching your ears.

Musical instruments do the same thing as your hands. They make molecules vibrate and send sound waves out. Then those waves surf through your ears into your brain.

Here is a picture of a sound wave.

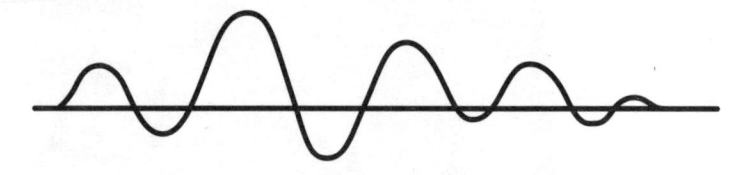

We use a special unit of measurement called hertz to work out how often a sound wave vibrates (what we call the 'frequency'). One hertz would be one vibration per second. Humans wouldn't be able to hear that, though. Humans can only hear sound when the sound wave vibrates between 20 and 20,000 times per second.

Your hand claps are about 2,500 hertz. That means if your clap was a second long, it would have sent out 2,500 sound waves. The number of waves sent out changes the note made. The higher the frequency (the more the wave vibrates), the higher the **PITCH** of the sound. The pitch is how high or low a note sounds. If I record Mark playing an A note on the saxophone, the wave looks like this:

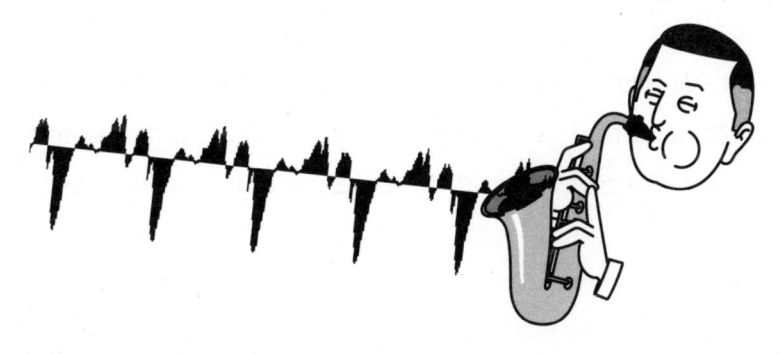

It goes up and down 440 times per second.

But just to make things more complicated, a sound wave might go up and down the same number of times but look very different. This is the sound wave of Joe playing an A on the trumpet:

It still goes up and down 440 times per second, but the wave has a different shape. And that is why it sounds different. The two instruments vibrate slightly differently, so their **WAVEFORMS** aren't the same. Then if they play these notes together, the wave combines and looks a bit like this:

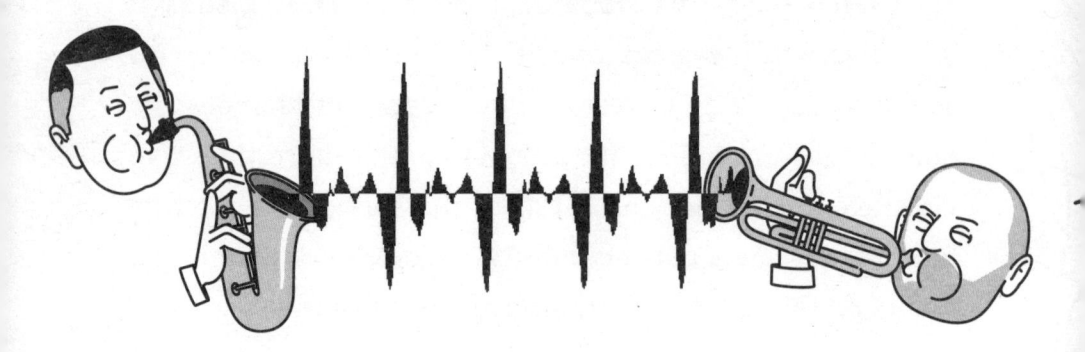

When a whole group play together, we hear a single waveform, which is a combination of all the different waves being created at the same time. Like this:

When lots of instruments play at the same time, the sound wave might *look* a bit messy but it will *sound* amazing.

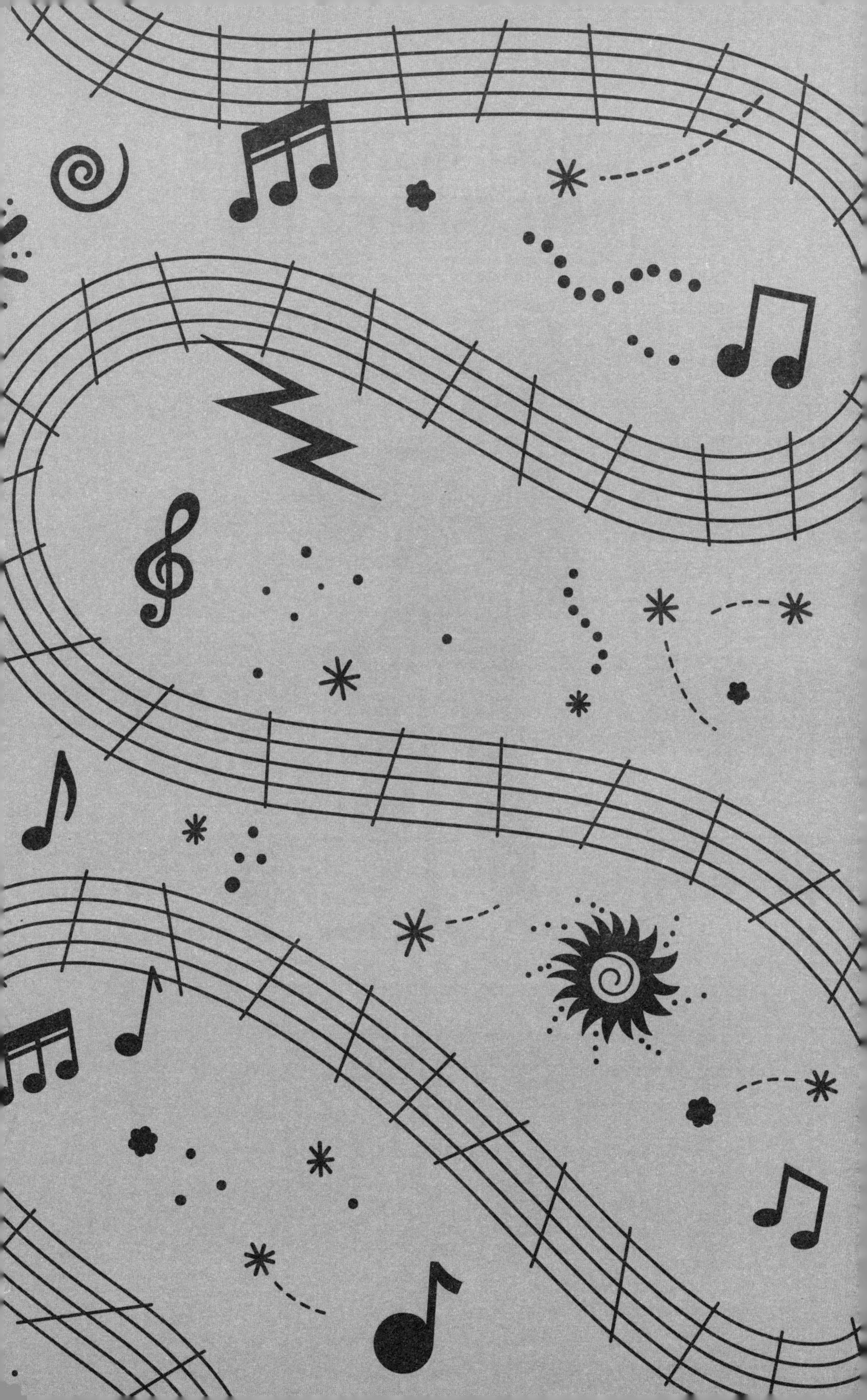

MUSICAL INSTRUMENTS HAVE FAMILIES TOO

When musical instruments were first made, we didn't have metal or plastic or computers, like we have now, so a lot of early instruments were made from bits of animals instead. The part of the drum that you hit used to be made from cow, goat, sheep or even buffalo skin. In fact, the earliest ones, made 30,000 years ago, were made of elephant skin. It's still called a skin in modern times, but these days it's made of plastic.

A few hundred years ago violin strings were made of 'catgut' (thought to be an abbreviation of 'cattle gut', as they came from the intestines of animals such as sheep). Bows for violins were (and still are) made from real horses' tails, bagpipes from pigs' bladders and trumpets from animal horns. Tortoise shells became excellent percussion instruments and seashells could be blown into or hit.

The good news is that most modern musical instruments are made of wood, metal, plastic or computers – so you can now take up an instrument without having to kill anything at all (though you may need to remove your neighbour's ears).

The instruments, like us, exist in families. They all fit into one of the five instrument families: strings, brass, woodwind, percussion and the keyboard family.

As we now know, all sound is caused by vibrating air waves and each family has found its own way of making these vibrations. So let's look at all 1,500 musical instruments. Or at least the big hitters. And the big blowers. And the big pluckers...

THE STRING FAMILY

> **DANGER RATING: LOW**
>
> THERE AREN'T MANY STRING-INSTRUMENT-RELATED DISASTERS. ONCE, THOUGH, AT THE SYDNEY OPERA HOUSE IN AUSTRALIA, A CHICKEN FELL FROM THE STAGE ON TO THE HEAD OF A CELLIST. HE MADE A FULL RECOVERY. AND SO DID THE CELLIST. SO STRING INSTRUMENTS ARE FAIRLY SAFE TO PLAY.

HELLO, STRING FAMILY!

The string family, as you might well expect, is full of instruments that have strings. The strings are rarely made of string, but don't let that confuse you. They're made of things like steel, nickel, brass, bronze or even nylon, but it's easier to pretend it's just string. The instruments themselves come in all different shapes and sizes, and their strings can be plucked or twanged or strummed or scraped with a bow, depending on what noise you want to make.

Imagine a cereal box with a hole in the front and some rubber bands stretched all the way round, which you can pluck. That's the sort of thing we're talking about, but just a little more expensive. When you move the rubber bands, or strings, this causes vibrations in the air. If you practise lots and learn the different techniques for moving the strings, you can control those vibrations to create lovely soft noises.

Within the string family are several smaller families. Let's start by meeting the violin family.

THE VIOLIN FAMILY

HELLO, VIOLIN FAMILY!

They don't say a lot, so we'll speak for them. Making music with a member of the violin family involves 'bowing' the strings, but you can also 'pluck' a string when required. Plucking is when you pull and release the string, twanging it like a rubber band. While bowing, in case you're wondering, involves rubbing or scraping the strings with a bow. And a bow (in case you're wondering again) is a stick with horse hair stretched from one end to another.

Yes, music is weird and that'll serve you right for wondering so much.

If the violin family were lined up for a family photo, the violin would be the child, as it's the smallest (it's the size of a cat). The parents – the next size up – are the viola and cello. And the grandparents – the biggest – are double basses. (We realize that in real life most grandparents aren't actually that much bigger than parents, but let's not worry too much about that.) String family gatherings happen in an orchestra, and these instruments play mainly classical music together. But violins and double basses are also used in jazz, folk and pop music. (More on these musical **GENRES** later!)

It's worth thinking about the size of the instrument when choosing one to play. Because they're so big, double basses and cellos rest on the floor while you play them, while violins and violas are tucked under your chin and held with one hand. If you go for a double bass, bear in mind that, with the case included, they weigh about 30 kg, which is the same as a grey wolf or an uninflated bouncy castle, so you will have a harder job getting it on the train or on the back of your bike.

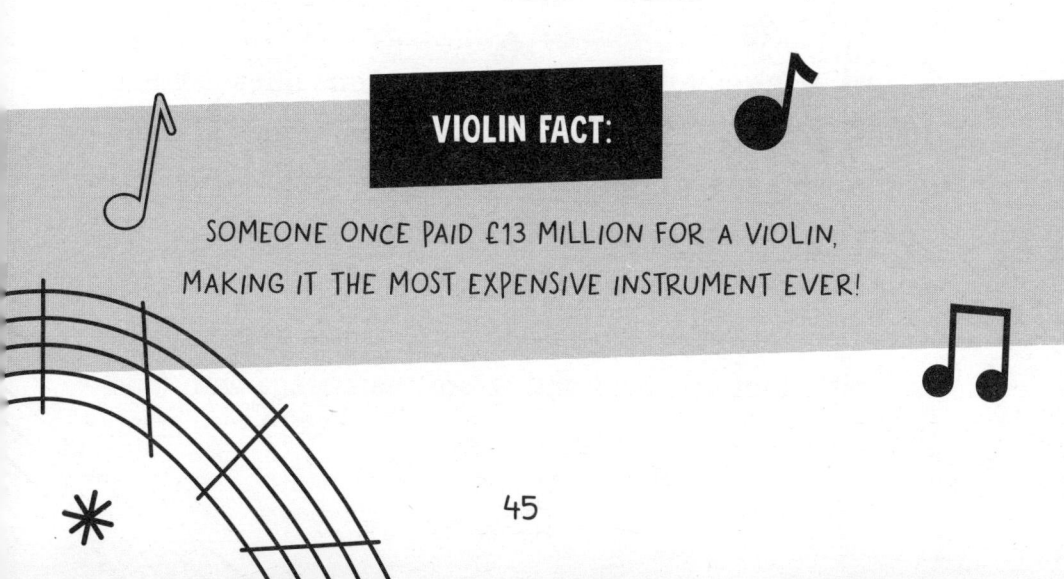

VIOLIN FACT:

SOMEONE ONCE PAID £13 MILLION FOR A VIOLIN, MAKING IT THE MOST EXPENSIVE INSTRUMENT EVER!

THE GUITAR FAMILY

HELLO, GUITAR FAMILY!

The guitar family are close cousins of the violin family. A basic guitar is larger than a violin and it has six strings instead of four.

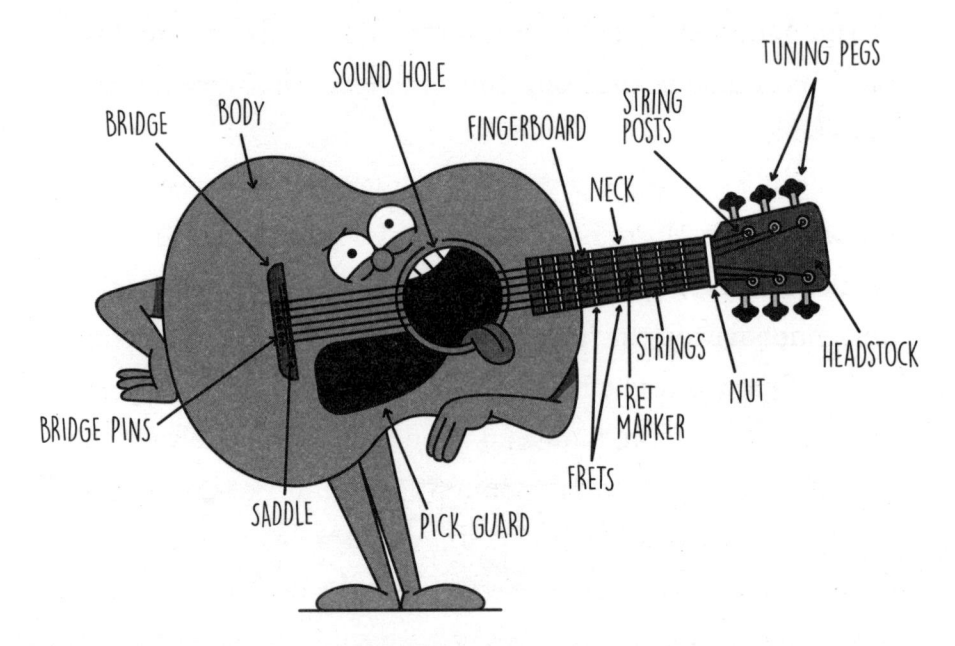

As well as the guitar itself, the ukulele, mandolin and banjo are all members of the guitar family. The strings of these instruments are strummed or plucked, a bit like chickens (apart from the strumming bit). Strumming is when you use your fingers to sweep over the strings to make the sound. Guitarists also often use a plectrum, which is a small piece of plastic that you hold and strum the strings with (and then lose every single time).

Acoustic guitars are made of wood and are hollow (which means they're empty inside), so try not to drop your sandwich through the hole. Electric guitars are also wooden but smaller, sleeker and often more colourful. The electric guitar is probably the coolest member of this cool family, mainly because you have to plug it into an amplifier that makes it really loud. Also, it doesn't have a hole in. If you play the electric guitar you need to give yourself an appropriately cool name like Slash, Dimebag, the Edge, Buckethead or Mark Brown.

If you don't have a cool name, you might be better off with a bass guitar. Particularly if you like your notes low and think you'd be happier playing just one note at a time. The bass has just four strings and plays the deepest notes and you have to try really hard to hear it being played in a song.

GUITAR FACT:

A MUSICIAN CALLED CHRIS BLACK LOVED HIS GUITAR SO MUCH THAT HE MARRIED IT IN 2001. THE INSTRUMENT WAS MADE BY A COMPANY CALLED FENDER SO CHRIS CALLED HER 'BRENDA THE FENDER'. ON HIS ALBUM, *CRAZY MAN CRAZY*, CHRIS EXPLAINED THAT HE AND BRENDA HAD BEEN 'DATING' FOR THIRTY-FIVE YEARS.

> If you want to know exactly how cool an electric guitar is, then the government have provided an official chart on the subject:

1

The electric guitar is twice as cool as an acoustic guitar.

2

The electric guitar is five times as cool as a tuba.

3

The electric guitar is two million times cooler than the recorder.

4

The electric guitar is so cool that you should always play it wearing jeans that have holes in.

Whether it's an electric guitar, a classical guitar or an acoustic guitar, some form of guitar is used in pretty much every musical genre from jazz to rock to soul to country and more. So we'd like to take a moment to show our appreciation for the guitar with a brief musical interlude. You can sing it right now, making up the tune as you go along:

This guitar is really versatile.
It can try its hand at every style.
It can be loud like a lorry at high speed
And quiet like a library where you read.

An electric guitar is called an axe.
You HAVE TO check out Jimi Hendrax.*
He could make it scream and make it roar
Then set it on fire and play some more.

A folk guitar is not on fire
But often played by a campfire.
You strum or pick and play sad songs.
In the chorus friends might sing along.

For classical guitar it's finger picking
So don't go eating greasy chicken!
It's calm and gentle, quite serene
And used in the folk, pop and country scene.

*We know it's 'Hendrix' but this rhymes better!

THE BRASS FAMILY

DANGER RATING: **HIGH**

WARNING: THESE INSTRUMENTS CAN GIVE YOU HEADACHES, BLACKOUTS, CARDIAC ARRHYTHMIAS, RESPIRATORY PROBLEMS AND MORE.

WE DON'T KNOW WHAT LOTS OF THESE WORDS MEAN BUT WE'RE PRETTY SURE THEY ARE ALL PAINFUL. YOU COULD LOOK THEM UP IN ANOTHER BOOK BUT WE WOULDN'T RECOMMEND THAT. YOU'RE SUPPOSED TO BE HERE LEARNING ABOUT MUSIC.

ALSO, IN 2010, A PROFESSIONAL TROMBONE PLAYER WAS SUFFERING FROM WHAT HE BELIEVED TO BE ASTHMA, WHICH IS A CONDITION THAT CAN MAKE IT DIFFICULT TO BREATHE. HOWEVER, DOCTORS COULD NOT FIND ANY TRACE OF THE CONDITION. WHILE ON HOLIDAY THE SYMPTOMS DISAPPEARED! ON RETURNING, HE HAD HIS TROMBONE INSPECTED AND FOUND OUT HE WAS ALLERGIC TO THE MOULD THAT WAS GROWING INSIDE THE INSTRUMENT. TURNS OUT THE DAMP, DARK CONDITIONS INSIDE A TROMBONE ARE IDEAL FOR GROWING FAIRLY UNPLEASANT BACTERIA! THE CONDITION WAS NAMED 'TROMBONE PLAYER'S LUNG'.

HELLO, BRASS FAMILY!

The brass family are another diverse family of instruments that come in many shapes and sizes. For example, an unravelled tuba is nearly 5.5 metres long, which is roughly the same as three Alex Hornes. While a cornet is only about 1.4 metres long.

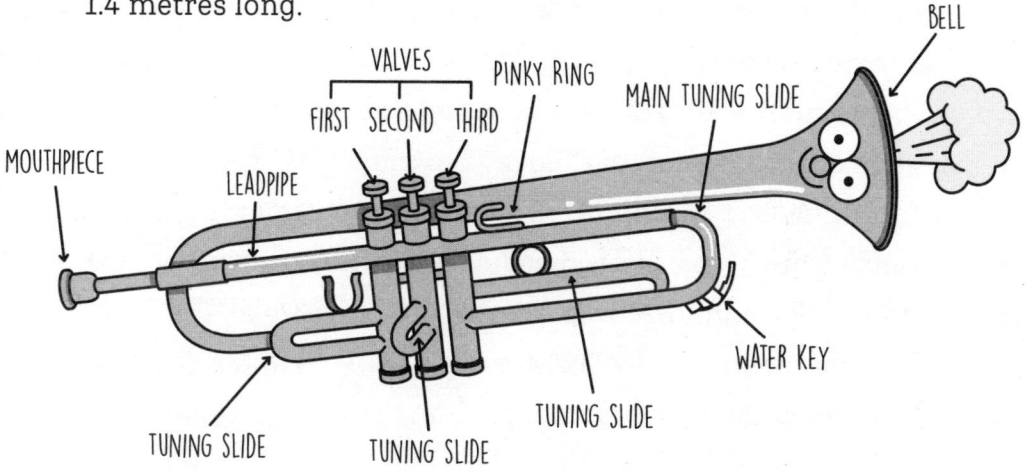

To make a sound with a brass instrument, someone must put their lips tightly on to the instrument's mouthpiece and blow raspberries. The vibration between the mouth and the mouthpiece pushes air through the instrument and results in a very loud noise. So really all a brass instrument does is amplify a raspberry.

> Are you telling me I make fart sounds with my mouth for a living?

If you've ever heard an elephant push air through its trunk, you'll know that they are the ultimate trumpeters. They don't get headaches and blackouts, though, because they are complete and utter naturals. You'll have to become an elephant if you want to play brass instruments safely. (Although it is worth noting that Joe is not a baby elephant – he's just a man who blows into a tube for a living.)

Elephants make trumpeting sounds to communicate with each other, and humans learned to play brass instruments for the same reason. At first these instruments weren't made from brass; instead people blew into naturally hollow items like animal horns, conch shells or wood that had been scraped out by little bugs called termites. Then a few thousand years ago the Romans started making their own horns using wood, bronze or silver. Like elephants, the Romans would use these 'trumpets' to pass messages on the battlefield, like 'Charge' or 'Attack' or 'That's enough war for one day' or 'Has Steve got the pork pies?'

Nowadays brass instruments are used for many different occasions and in lots of genres. Both past and current musicians, including legendary English rock band The Beatles, English singer and songwriter Amy Winehouse, global superstar Bruno Mars and American singer Beyoncé (the queen of modern music) feature brass sections in their music. These instruments are also used to play fanfares to announce the arrival of a member of a royal family or to open an important ceremony or a new chip shop. Our trumpeter, Joe, once played for the arrival of King Charles at Buckingham Palace.

Here are the main brass instruments in size order:

TRUMPET   FRENCH HORN   TROMBONE   TUBA

BRASS FACT:

A TROMBONIST WILL WHISPER, ON AVERAGE, SEVEN JOKES TO A FELLOW TROMBONIST DURING EVERY PERFORMANCE.

THE WOODWIND FAMILY

DANGER RATING: **LEMON AND HERB**

THESE INSTRUMENTS ARE SIMPLY NOT DANGEROUS. YOU DON'T HAVE TO WEAR A HELMET TO PLAY ONE AND THEY'RE NOT PARTICULARLY SHARP OR HEAVY. HAVING SAID THAT, IF YOU BLOW TOO HARD ON A SAXOPHONE, YOU MIGHT GET A HERNIA, WHICH IS A MEDICAL ISSUE TO LOOK UP IF YOU'RE FEELING BRAVE.

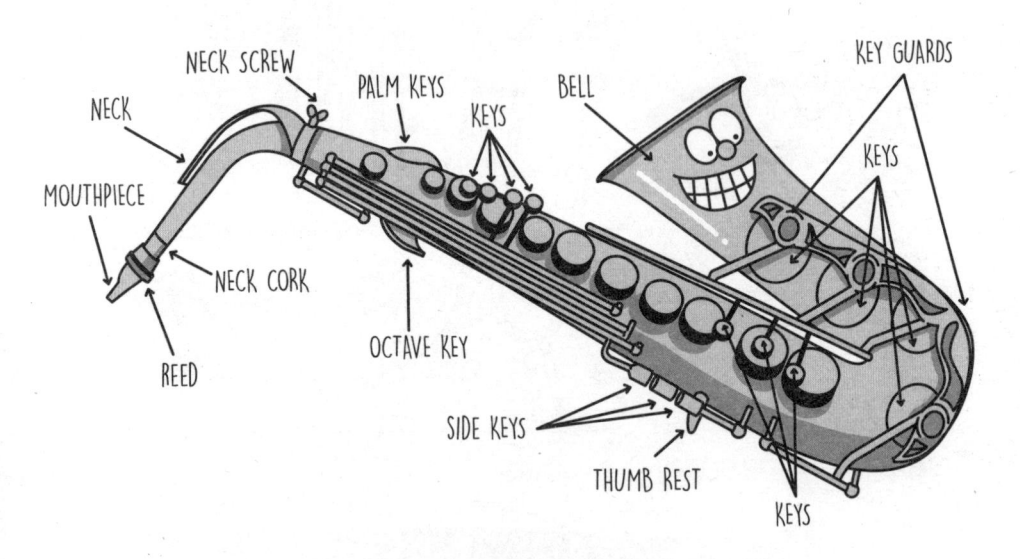

HELLO, WOODWIND FAMILY!

What do you get if you combine wind and wood? Either a lot of trees falling down or some sweet-sounding music. Let's have a look at the second of these options.

Saxophones, oboes, bassoons and flutes are the sorts of instruments that fall into the woodwind category. Mark plays these instruments. He's a woodwinder. They are called woodwind instruments, rather than brass instruments, because traditionally these instruments were made of wood, but now many are made from metal and plastic.

Woodwind instruments make their wonderful noise in a couple of different ways. Have you ever made a sound by blowing over the top of a glass bottle? Well, that's pretty much what you do with these instruments. And it sounds the same too.

Most woodwind instruments have a reed that the musician blows into. What's a reed? Good question. A reed is a thin strip of bamboo or plastic that you find in the mouthpiece of an instrument. When you blow down a woodwind instrument, it's the reed that vibrates to create the sound that travels through the rest of the instrument and out of the other end. Thank you, reeds.

The flute is one of the few woodwind instruments that doesn't have a reed. Clarinets and saxophones are called single-reed instruments because they have one reed each. Oboes and bassoons are called double-reed instruments. I imagine you can guess why. These instruments make their sound by someone like Mark blowing on to one of the reeds, which then vibrates against the other one.

You can get a range of sounds from woodwind instruments. They can growl like a proud lion, cry or snuffle like a lonely little boy or bark like a hungry dog – and all in the same jazz solo! They are controlled in the same way as a human voice, using breath, lips and throat, or what is called the 'BLT'. This gives their sound a human quality that makes them expressive and useful background music for sad grown-up TV shows.

Most wind instruments live in an orchestra and sit in front of the brass section. Here you'll find:

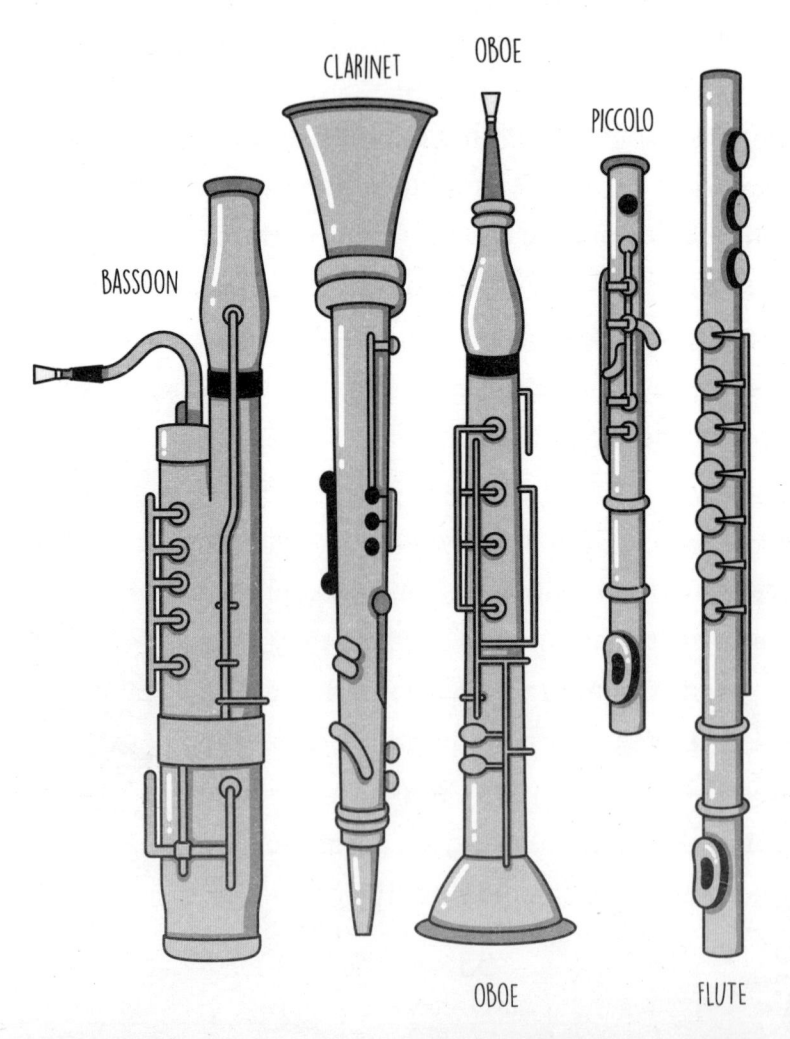

BASSOON CLARINET OBOE PICCOLO

OBOE FLUTE

WOODWIND FACT:

THE SAXOPHONE IS THE NEW GUY ON THE BLOCK IN THE WOODWIND FAMILY AND WAS INVENTED BY MR ADOLPHE SAX IN 1846, ABOUT 500 YEARS AFTER THE RECORDER. HE REALIZED THAT MAKING THESE SINGLE-REED INSTRUMENTS FROM BRASS RATHER THAN WOOD WOULD MAKE THEM FAR LOUDER AND THEREFORE USEFUL IN MARCHING BANDS.

The saxophone was welcomed by the cool jazz musicians of 1920s America, who used a lot of saxophone in their music. If you want to hear a bit of that, look up American saxophonists Sidney Bechet and Coleman Hawkins. These smartly dressed guys were followed by men with long curly hair, like Kenny G and Clarence Clemons, who started playing saxophone solos in eighties pop music. Ideally to play the saxophone you would need to have a jazzy name like Lockjaw or Yardbird or Cannonball or Mark.

THE PERCUSSION FAMILY

> **DANGER RATING: MEDIUM**
>
> THE ONLY INSTRUMENT WITH WHICH YOU ARE ARMED WITH A STICK OR MALLET. IN FACT, PERCUSSIONISTS ARE USUALLY MORE OF A DANGER TO OTHERS THAN THEMSELVES.

HELLO, PERCUSSION FAMILY!

At last a group of instruments that...

- Everyone can play without having to put things in or near their mouths.
- Anyone can get involved in, using whatever they can find lying around.
- Will drive your parents mad within just a few minutes.

Percussion is all about hitting things with other things. The first of those 'things' is normally drums or cymbals, but you can hit pots and pans, walls, tables or fancy antique vases. The second 'thing', which does the hitting, is normally drumsticks, but can easily be hands, balls, spoons, brushes or bats. Have a look around you right now and see if you can find a thing to hit and a thing to do the hitting with (please don't use a person for either 'thing'). Then turn on the radio and play along to the music with your objects. Congratulations! You're a percussionist!

One of the oldest percussion instruments we know about is 70,000 years old and was found in Belgium. It was made from mammoth bones! Later, around 5500 BCE, drums were being made from alligator skin. This happened first in China and soon spread right across Asia. Drums then became popular across Africa between 1000 and 500 BCE, and they found their way to Europe by 150 BCE. Initially, like brass instruments, they were mainly used for communication, as a way of sending messages to nearby communities. If mobile phones had been invented earlier, we'd have far fewer musical instruments to choose from...

In case you're wondering how drums actually work, here's the science bit: a drum is a hollow tube, or **SHELL** if you want to use the fancy word. It has a skin stretched tightly over one end, sometimes both. When you strike the drum skin with a stick or your hand, the air in the drum shell underneath vibrates and creates a much louder sound. So the big bit of the drum amplifies the noise of the strike. You can change the pitch of a drum by tightening or loosening the skin.

PERCUSSION FACT:

THE WORD 'DRUM' ORIGINATES FROM THE WORD 'BUM'. THE BUM HAS BEEN SCIENTIFICALLY PROVEN TO MAKE THE MOST MUSICAL SOUNDS OF ALL THE BODY PARTS.

To keep things simple, let's divide percussion into **THE DRUM KIT** and **THE REST**.

THE DRUM KIT

The first use of a drum kit was in the late 1800s. Before this loads of different people had to play the different parts of the kit. One person was in charge of the bass drum, someone else hit the snare and another person bashed all the cymbals. Then along came a show-off called Edward 'Dee Dee' Chandler, an American drummer who cleverly arranged the drums in a way that meant he could reach them all at the same time. Good old Dee Dee. Soon after that someone else invented the foot pedal for playing the bass drum (but they didn't have a good nickname like Dee Dee so we don't know who that was).

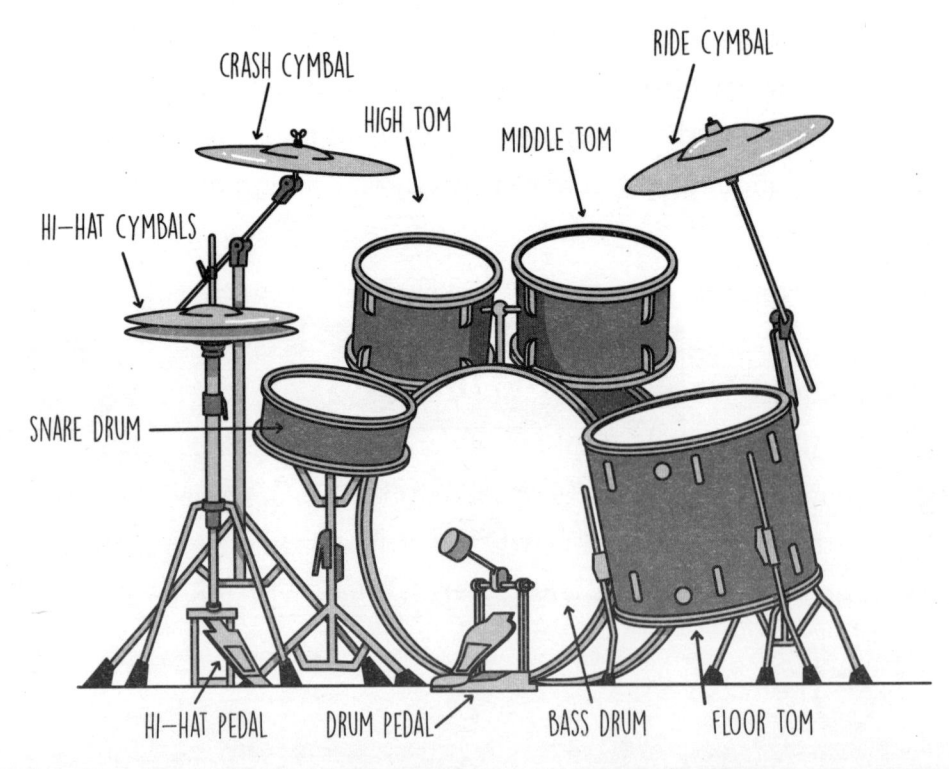

CRASH CYMBAL
HIGH TOM
MIDDLE TOM
RIDE CYMBAL
HI-HAT CYMBALS
SNARE DRUM
HI-HAT PEDAL
DRUM PEDAL
BASS DRUM
FLOOR TOM

Pop and rock bands nearly always feature a drum kit. People often call the drummer the 'backbone' or 'engine room' of a band, and that's because the music would either become very floppy or stop completely without one.

The sound of the drum is very helpful for keeping everyone else in a band playing in time. The drum kit lays down the 'beat' or 'groove' of the music and keeps the musicians together. Our own drummer, Ben, sees himself as a sheepdog, constantly nipping at our heels to keep the band in check. Although this may also be because he gets cross when he's hungry and he likes to snack on our ankles.

As well as whacking things, counting is one of the most important skills to have as a drummer. You'll need to be able to count up to at least four, sometimes even seven, if you want to make it as a pro. The drummer in a band counts the other band members in, and the timing and speed of this lets everyone know when to start blowing, plucking or hitting their instruments and how fast to do so.

The drummer's count in at the start of a tune also tells the band what time signature they will be playing in. A time signature refers to how many beats there are in a bar of music. And a bar of music is a box that organizes written music into smaller sections. Each bar in a song usually has the same number of beats. Most of the music we play in the Horne Section has either three or four beats in a bar.

Let's practise playing these two time signatures so you can see what we mean!

1 Put three fingers on a table and tap them in turn at a comfortable speed, or **TEMPO** as we call it in music.

2 Say the phrase below, with every word in time with each finger tap.

'I AM GREAT – THIS IS ME – GREAT I AM – THIS IS THREE.'

Well done. You ARE great and you are playing music with three beats in a bar!

3 Rest time. Just relax and wallow in your glory.

Now let's try four beats in a bar.

1 Pop another finger on the table.

2 Say this phrase with each finger tap.

'WOW! I'M SO GOOD – KNOW YOU WANT MORE – I KNEW I COULD – THIS BAR HAS FOUR.'

You absolute legend. You've done it again. You're playing music with four beats in a bar.

3 More wallowing please.

OK, just a couple more drum terms now:

1. A **DRUM FILL** is a short flurry of banging from the drummer between the lines of a song, often finished by a crash on a cymbal. Imagine a drum kit falling down the stairs and you've got a pretty good idea of how this sounds.

2. A **DRUM PHIL** is someone called Phil who plays the drums.

3. A **DRUM DEBBIE** is someone called Debbie who plays the drums.

THE REST — TUNED PERCUSSION

Have you ever listened to a xylophone, glockenspiel or vibraphone? No, this isn't a spelling test, it's a list of very big, tuneful percussion instruments. You still hit them but they make musical notes rather than just going *donk* or *tish*.

> I am a proper musician!

You'll find these instruments at the very back of an orchestra, joined by the timpani or kettle drums, which are absolutely massive and go *boing*.

You might have heard of music called salsa, samba, bossa nova, tango and rumba. They come under the umbrella of Latin American music, which is a type of folk music originating from Central and South America – hot, colourful places like Cuba, Brazil, Argentina and Mexico. These vibrant, exciting musical styles put percussion front and centre!

Brazilian carnivals feature huge marching bands called *baterias* and can have dozens of percussionists as well as singers and brass sections. The most common tuned percussion instruments here are congas, bongos, shakers, tambourines and cowbells, and the dancing is just as important as the music itself.

THE KEYBOARD FAMILY

DANGER RATING: **MILD**

UNLESS A PIANO FALLS ON TOP OF YOU, IN WHICH CASE, MASSIVE.

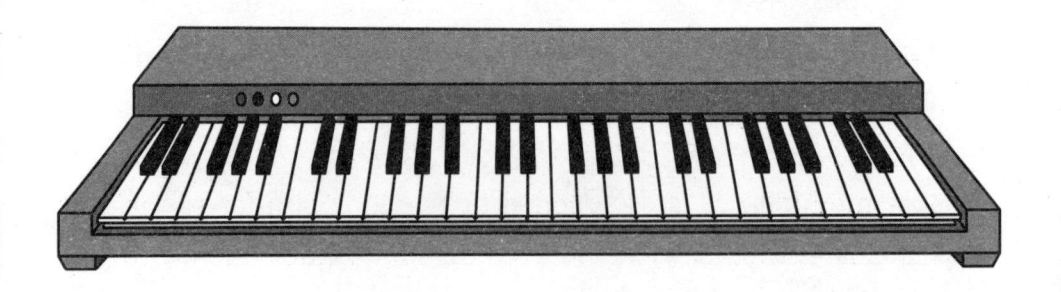

KEYBOARD FACT:

YAMAHA IS THE BIGGEST MANUFACTURER OF KEYBOARDS, MAKING 54% OF ALL THE PORTABLE KEYBOARDS SOLD IN 2019. THE COMPANY STARTED MAKING THEM IN 1900, THEN DECIDED TO PRODUCE MOTORBIKES TOO IN THE 1950S. THEY'VE RECENTLY STARTED MAKING ROBOTS AS WELL, SO THEY'RE DEFINITELY ONE OF THE COOLEST COMPANIES IN THE WORLD.

HELLO, KEYBOARD FAMILY!

The main instruments you'll find in the keyboard family are the piano, the organ, the harpsichord, the accordion and the electronic synthesizer. Pianos are everywhere: schools, churches, hotels and sometimes even railway stations. There's even a piano on the moon. Why? Because pianos are very useful.

A single piano can do the job of an entire band or orchestra. It can provide beautiful notes, melodies and rhythms, and play all the music! If you don't believe me, try having a sing-along party gathered round a bassoon.

Most members of the keyboard family look similar to the piano. They all have a keyboard made up of black and white keys that play different notes. In some cases, though, the keyboard can be made up of buttons, and playing these feels more like using a calculator.

Playing the instruments of the keyboard family is a little more complicated than banging a tortoise with a stick. Here's how they use keys to make sound:

PIANO – THE KEY MOVES A SMALL HAMMER THAT HITS A STRING.

HARPSICHORD – THE KEY MOVES A SMALL HOOK THAT PLUCKS A STRING.

ORGAN – THE KEY MOVES A SLIDER THAT ALLOWS AIR TO PASS THROUGH A PIPE (SO THE SOUND IS MADE IN A SIMILAR WAY TO A FLUTE).

ELECTRONIC SYNTHESIZER – SYNTHESIZERS DON'T PHYSICALLY CREATE VIBRATIONS WITH HAMMERS OR HOOKS LIKE THE OTHER MEMBERS OF ITS FAMILY. INSTEAD, WHEN THE BUTTONS ARE PRESSED, AN **ELECTRICAL SIGNAL** IS PASSED TO AN AMPLIFIER. THE AMPLIFIER SENDS THE SIGNAL THROUGH A SPEAKER TO CREATE VIBRATIONS IN THE AIR THAT WE HEAR AS SOUND.

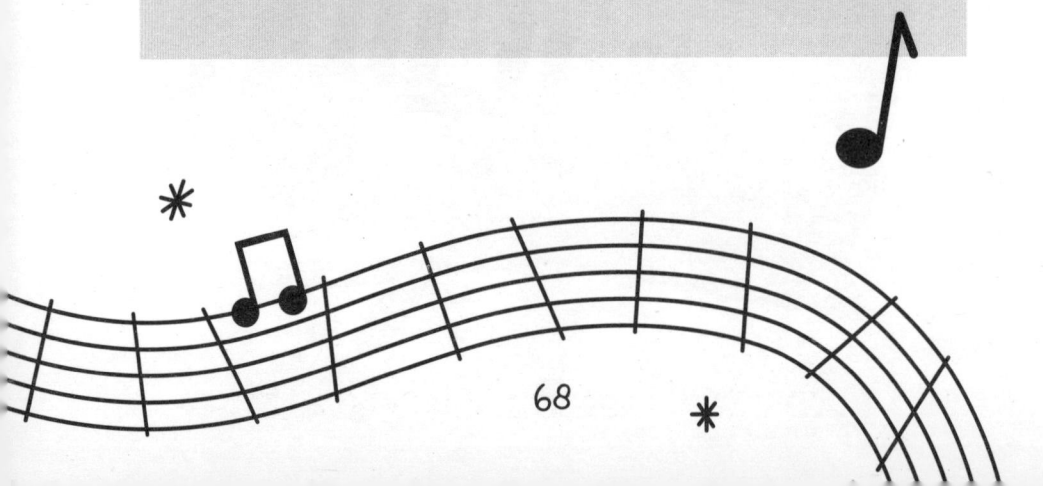

Before we end this chapter we should mention elephants again. In the brass section we talked about elephants being natural brass players, but they have a close link with pianos too. A grand piano weighs the same as a female elephant, so if you see an elephant on one end of a see-saw and a piano on the other, the see-saw will be completely flat.

There's also a man called Paul Barton who plays piano for elephants around the world. In 2011 Paul was working as a piano teacher in Thailand when he visited a sanctuary for old and injured elephants. Being a musician, he asked if he could play piano for them. As soon as he did so, the nearest elephant stopped what he was doing, stood still and listened.

Every time Paul played, the elephant curled the tip of his trunk into his mouth and stayed like that, calmly, until the piece was finished. Since then, Paul has regularly played for them, raising money for their care and calming the gentle giants. Have a look on YouTube to see an eighty-year-old blind elephant listening to him play. It's one of the best demonstrations of the power and magic of music we've ever seen. If only all our audiences were elephants.

THE INSTRUMENT IN YOUR MOUTH RIGHT NOW

From the day you were born you started practising an instrument. A unique instrument you will have for all your life: your voice. You keep this instrument safe and hidden. You carry it around all day. Inside a box. In your throat. This mysterious box is called your **VOICE BOX**, or if you are a doctor (or want to impress someone) you might call it your larynx.

Inside your larynx is where you keep your vocal cords. When you speak, sing or shout at a bus for not stopping, air passes through your larynx, making your vocal cords vibrate. With enough pressure coming from air underneath your vocal cords, the bus driver might just hear you. Although we can't promise they will stop. In fairness to the bus driver, they should only stop at a designated bus stop. You shouldn't really shout at buses.

Forget bone flutes and dusty drums – your voice is the oldest instrument in the world. Ever. From operas to burps, people have been making wonderful sounds with their vocal cords for hundreds of thousands of years!

At first there were no words said or songs sung. Language didn't even exist. The earliest sounds are said to have probably been made by people copying sounds heard in nature, and may have included grunts, cries, howls and whoops. (If you listen to rock, heavy metal and even some Horne Section songs, it would seem little has changed.)

Eventually people began using their voices to sing sweet tunes. Just like any other musician, people spend years practising singing and using their voice as an instrument. It is, without a doubt, the cheapest, most compact and easiest to move of all the instruments in this book. So maybe it's worth considering if you don't quite have the space for that full-size church organ in your parents' sitting room.

MUSICAL TASKS

MUSICAL TASK NUMBER TWO

Make a musical instrument from something edible.

Maybe you could cut holes in a cucumber and make a flute, or hit a packet of crisps, turning it into a percussion instrument. Using your new instrument, play a recognizable tune, then eat your musical instrument.

Best edible instrument wins.

YOUR TIME STARTS NOW.

THE LIES!

It is not true that I, Alex Horne, cannot play a single instrument. I used to play French horn actually. I chose it because it had the same name as me, but that turned out to be a bad plan. The French horn is REALLY difficult. Also, if everyone chose instruments based on their surnames, no one would ever play the xylophone again.

The government haven't really provided an official chart on how cool the electric guitar is. But if they did, it would look exactly like the one next to Mark.

The word 'drum' sadly doesn't come from the word 'bum'. Instead it's related to an old Dutch word *tromme* and simply sounds like the noise you make when you hit one.

Trombonists don't whisper, on average, seven jokes to a fellow trombonist during every performance.

There isn't a piano on the moon, as far as we know.

CHAPTER

THREE

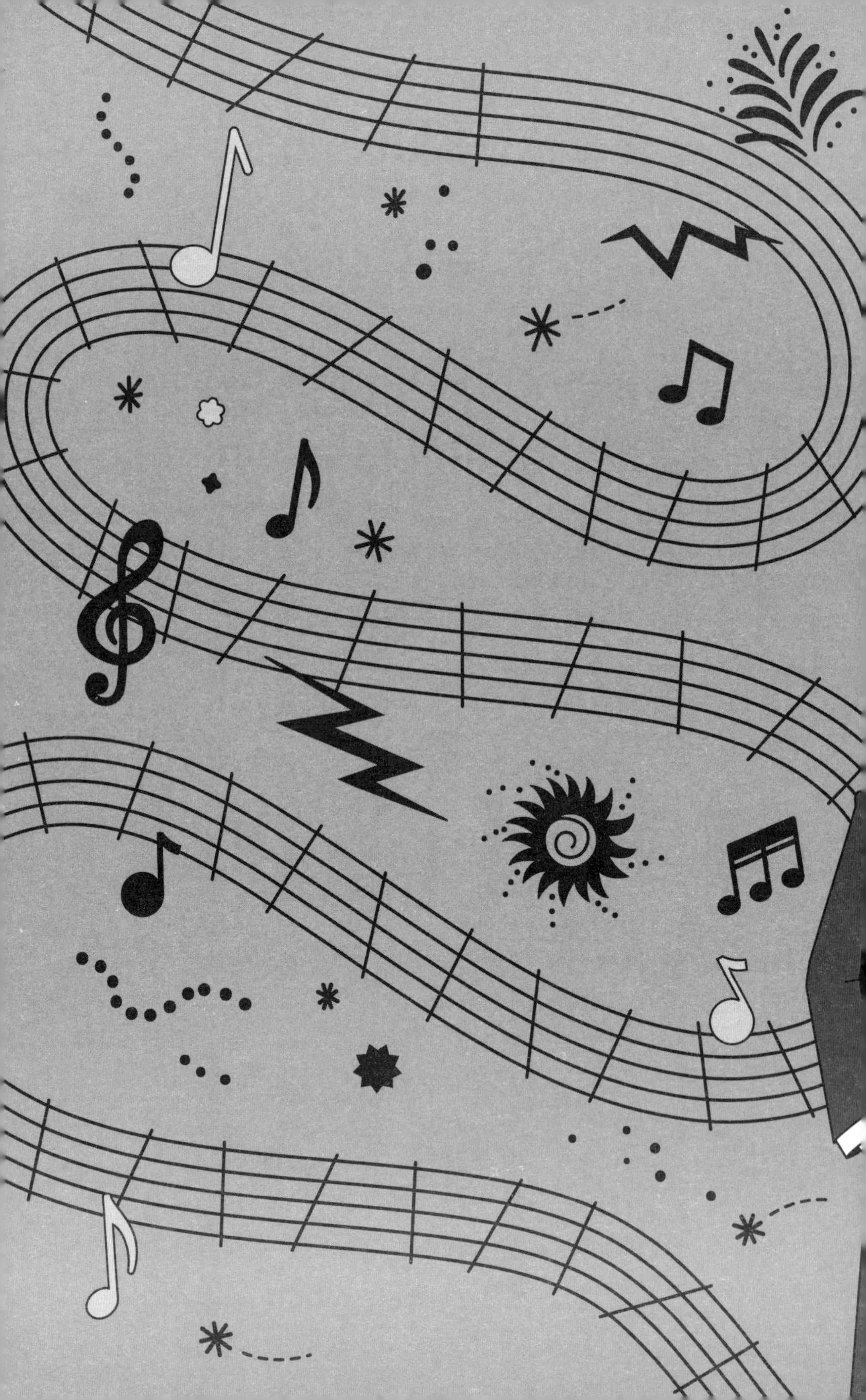

WHAT DO ALL THE DOTS AND SQUIGGLES MEAN?

We now know about the different musical instrument families. Well done, us! But when you see an orchestra or band play, the musicians don't just have all those tubas and flutes and violins. They often have stands in front of them too. Music stands. So, what are they hiding?

Luckily for you I've done some research and can now tell you the answer. Some are definitely watching football matches on iPads, but most musicians have sheet music on their stands. Sheet music is like a book but with musical notes instead of letters. It's what musicians use to learn and play music. Often they have many pages of sheet music. Sometimes many pages for just one piece.

Musicians pop the sheet music they want to play on their music stands and then all blow, pluck or hit different notes on their instruments based on when the dots and symbols on the page tell them to. Not all musicians use sheet music, but it is often the case for orchestral music and anything a bit complicated that musicians have trouble remembering.

Rock and pop bands don't tend to have music stands (maybe because they think it will ruin their cool image). Although they do sometimes write the words or directions for a song where the audience won't see them, whether that's on the back of their hands or, if they have small hands, on the face of someone sitting in the front row.

THE FIRST-EVER WRITTEN MUSIC

Around 60,000 years before Mr Sax invented his saxophone, a Neanderthal was playing a flute, which you'll remember was made from a bear bone, in a cave in Slovenia. That's the oldest instrument ever found and, to put that time in perspective, it's roughly 10,470 guinea pigs' lives ago.

> That's 3,132,000 Wednesdays ago. Whether you count it in Wednesdays or guinea pigs, that's a really old flute.

Sadly no accompanying sheet music or cave paintings were found, and this means we can only imagine what banging dance anthems those Neanderthals put out.

It wasn't until around 2000 BCE (10,121 guinea pigs later) that some people started to think writing music down might actually be a good idea. A small slab of clay with some musical notation scratched on it was found in a place called Nippur, which is now in Iraq. We don't know who wrote it or what exactly it means but this is the earliest-known written music. It's hard to read but it does seem to be a single melody and isn't considered a complete tune. So nothing to make a song and dance about.

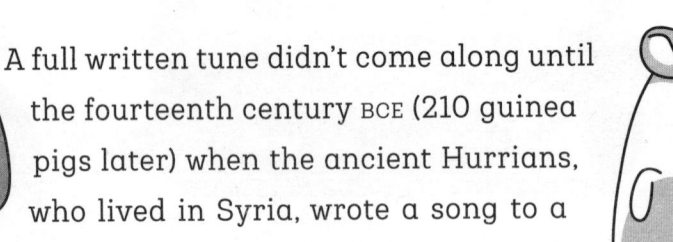

A full written tune didn't come along until the fourteenth century BCE (210 guinea pigs later) when the ancient Hurrians, who lived in Syria, wrote a song to a goddess called Nikkal. They hadn't progressed much in the writing department so this was also written on a clay tablet. Helpfully, though, the Hurrians also included instructions on how to play the music on a nine-stringed instrument called a lyre. Hurray, Hurrians!

One hundred and eighteen guinea pigs later (1332 BCE) saw the reign of Pharaoh Tutankhamun in Egypt. Also known to us these days as King Tut, he ruled the country from when he was eight or nine years old and is still really famous because his tomb was discovered completely intact thousands of years later in 1922. In this enormous royal grave two trumpets were discovered. Unfortunately we have no idea what music was played on these instruments. It seems Tutankhamun hadn't followed in the Hurrians' footsteps, and no helpful instructions had been left for us.

Toot-toot-ankhamun?

TODAY'S WRITTEN MUSIC

Soon humans realized that writing music on clay tablets was expensive, impractical and also awkward for children to fit in their school bags. So now we use either paper or a computer. We tend to find clay more suitable for tiles, toilets, teacups and televisions.

BONUS MUSICAL TOILET FACT:

AMERICAN SINGER-SONGWRITER LIONEL RICHIE WROTE THE SONG 'LADY', WHICH WAS RECORDED BY A SINGER NAMED KENNY ROGERS, IN THE TOILET OF A RECORDING STUDIO IN 1980. IT'S NOW LISTED AS NUMBER 67 IN BILLBOARD'S GREATEST OF ALL TIME HOT 100 SONGS. IT'S A VERY ROMANTIC SONG ABOUT FINALLY MEETING THE ONE YOU LOVE, WITH NOT SO MUCH AS A MENTION OF RUNNING OUT OF TOILET PAPER WHEN YOU NEED IT MOST.

WHY WRITE MUSIC DOWN?

When you read a book you are discovering what a person thought about something. From wizards to dinosaurs to murder mysteries and chipolatas, there is a book for every occasion, and many were written hundreds, even thousands, of years ago. And because they were written down, the authors' words can be passed on for generations to come. It's the same with songs. When music is written down it can continue to be enjoyed by people and played long into the future by other musicians.

OK, GREAT, BUT *HOW* DO I WRITE MUSIC DOWN?

It might surprise you to find out that the current method for writing down music – the method used in schools, orchestras and bands all around the Western world today – owes a great deal to the church. Or at least the church between the years 500 and 1400.

Back then **COMPOSERS** (people who write music) in these places of worship decided it would be good if all the churches could sing the same songs. They called it ecclesiastical uniformity but if you say that phrase to 99% of people, they won't know what you mean. (Go for it and watch them pretend to understand.) The main thing you need to know is that these musical trailblazers wrote their songs down on paper and distributed them far and wide, travelling by horse or even on foot. It was hard work but effective.

So how did they write the music? Well, Western music is written on a 'stave'. A stave is five horizontal lines. You've probably heard your music teacher waffling on about these.

Forget the waffle! Here's the best way to picture one if you have never seen one before. Imagine a five-bar fence crossing a field of daffodils with a small stream running through it. Got it? Good. Now forget the river, daffodils and field.

Just imagine the fence. This is your stave, and each line or space on this five-bar fence represents a specific pitch on a given instrument (or a different drum if you are looking at sheet music for drum kits).

Composers hang black dots on the fence or squash them in between the bars. These dots are called notes. Musicians look at the position of the dots, and these tell them what notes to blow, hit or pluck on their instruments, and the type of dot tells them how long to blow, hit or pluck them for. The higher the dot is on the stave, the higher the note you're meant to play. And all the notes have letters to tell them apart, starting from A and going to G. A dot on the bottom row is an E, a dot in the gap above that is an F, then G, then A and all the way up to an F on the top rung.

If you look at a piano, you'll see there are lots of white keys (fifty-two, in fact). But how does that work if we only use seven letters for our notes? Don't panic! All that happens is that after G we go back to A again. That's because every eighth note sounds the same, just higher or lower (in the same way as red tomatoes all look the same, just smaller or bigger). If there is a piano at your school, play around with the keys to see how you can get high As and low As, very high Ds and very low Ds and so on. We call each group of eight notes an octave.

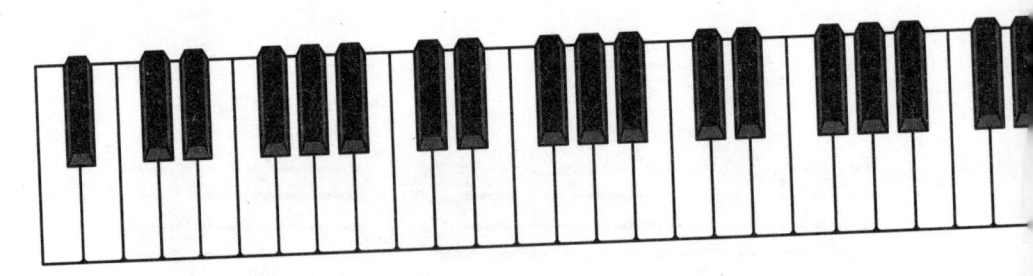

What about the thirty-six black keys on a piano? Good point and well counted. This is where it does get a bit more fiddly. There are actually other notes between the letters, which means there are more than seven different sounds. These extra notes are called 'sharps' and 'flats'. 'Sharps' are not as dangerous as they sound. To 'sharpen' a note means to make it slightly higher in pitch, so A sharp is a tiny bit higher than A.

'Flats' are not as boring as they sound. To 'flatten' a note is to make it a tiny bit lower. So A flat is slightly lower than A. If you happen to live in a flat you could sing 'welcome to a flat' on the note A flat every time you answer the door. And all this means that an octave contains twelve different notes in total, once you've added in the sharps and flats.

Some instruments, like the piano, harp and the marimba (basically an overgrown xylophone), use two staves for their written music. This is because they have too many notes to fit on one stave. They have a stave for the high notes and a stave for the low notes. So, if you chopped a piano in half (please don't try this at school), all the notes from the mangled right-hand side of the piano generally sit on the top stave and the destroyed remaining left-hand side of the piano has its deeper-sounding notes drawn on the lower stave.

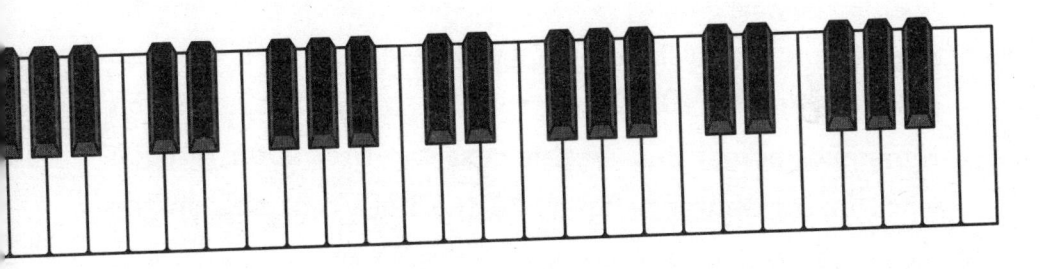

Sometimes the composer doesn't want the musician to play anything at all. If this is the case, you would see a symbol for a 'rest' on the stave. This doesn't mean the composer wants you to have a lie-down or a glass of squash; they just want you to be quiet for a part of the song until you are told to play some more notes. If there is time to have a glass of squash, then just make sure you keep it well hidden behind your music stand.

SO HOW EXACTLY DO I READ THIS MUSICAL NOTATION?

If you've had musical instrument lessons at home or in school, you may well have been taught a phrase like 'Every good boy deserves fun'. If you've not had musical instrument lessons, you're probably thinking *don't girls deserve fun too?*

The reason we say 'Every good boy deserves fun' is that the phrase is a **MNEMONIC** – a group of words that helps you remember something. In this case the first letter of each word in the sentence refers to the note that sits on the stave, going from the bottom to top. Every = E, Good = G, Boy = B and so on. There is also a mnemonic for the gaps in the stave: F A C E.

Before we move on I must ask you a very important question. Do you like eating cabbage? Of course not! None of us like eating cabbage either. It's horrible stuff. But we do like eating it WITH OUR EARS. Now before you stuff a cabbage into your ear canals (please don't do this) consider doing it like we do – musically.

We have produced our own method for making up and writing music based purely on food and the places where people make food. Once you have learned the notes on the stave you can play the most wonderful tunes using groups of notes like **EGG, BEEF, CAFE** and, yes, **CABBAGE**! If you don't have an instrument at home, why not borrow one from school or a friend, and work out how to play each of these notes, then play out all these words?

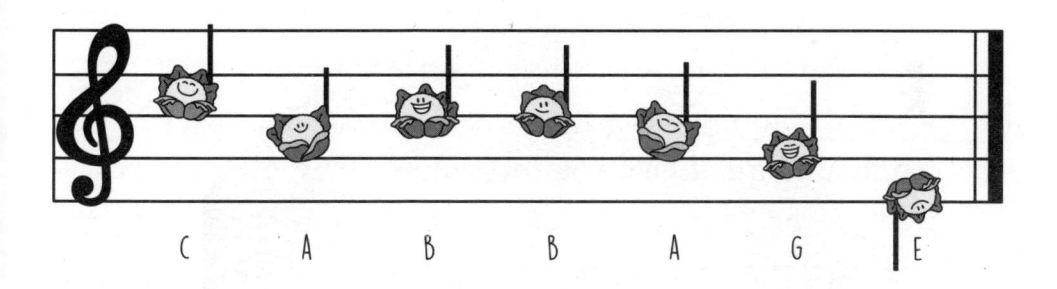

C A B B A G E

We know how cabbage tastes (YUCK!) but how does it sound? (YUMMY!) so pick up an instrument and stuff a load of cabbage into your ears right now.

Once you have these notes under your fingers, see if you can create your own rhythms to the melody. Try making something you can really tap your feet to.

Then why not explore other beautiful words on your instrument and try writing your own tune using note letters? DEFACED and BAGGAGE both create some interesting melodies.

We once composed a song about a sad lonely BEE named BAGFACE who unfortunately ended up DEAD. Using just seven letters to write **LYRICS** is a bit limiting but it's also really fun and, as we now know, every good boy (and girl) deserves some of that.

There you have it. Reading music is brilliant for your brain. Like sudokus or crosswords, it's a really rewarding and satisfying thing to be able to do, and it has been proven to sharpen your mind, boost your self-esteem, improve your coordination and help you feel calmer. Plus, once you've cracked the code, you could join a band, a choir or an orchestra and make loads of new friends!

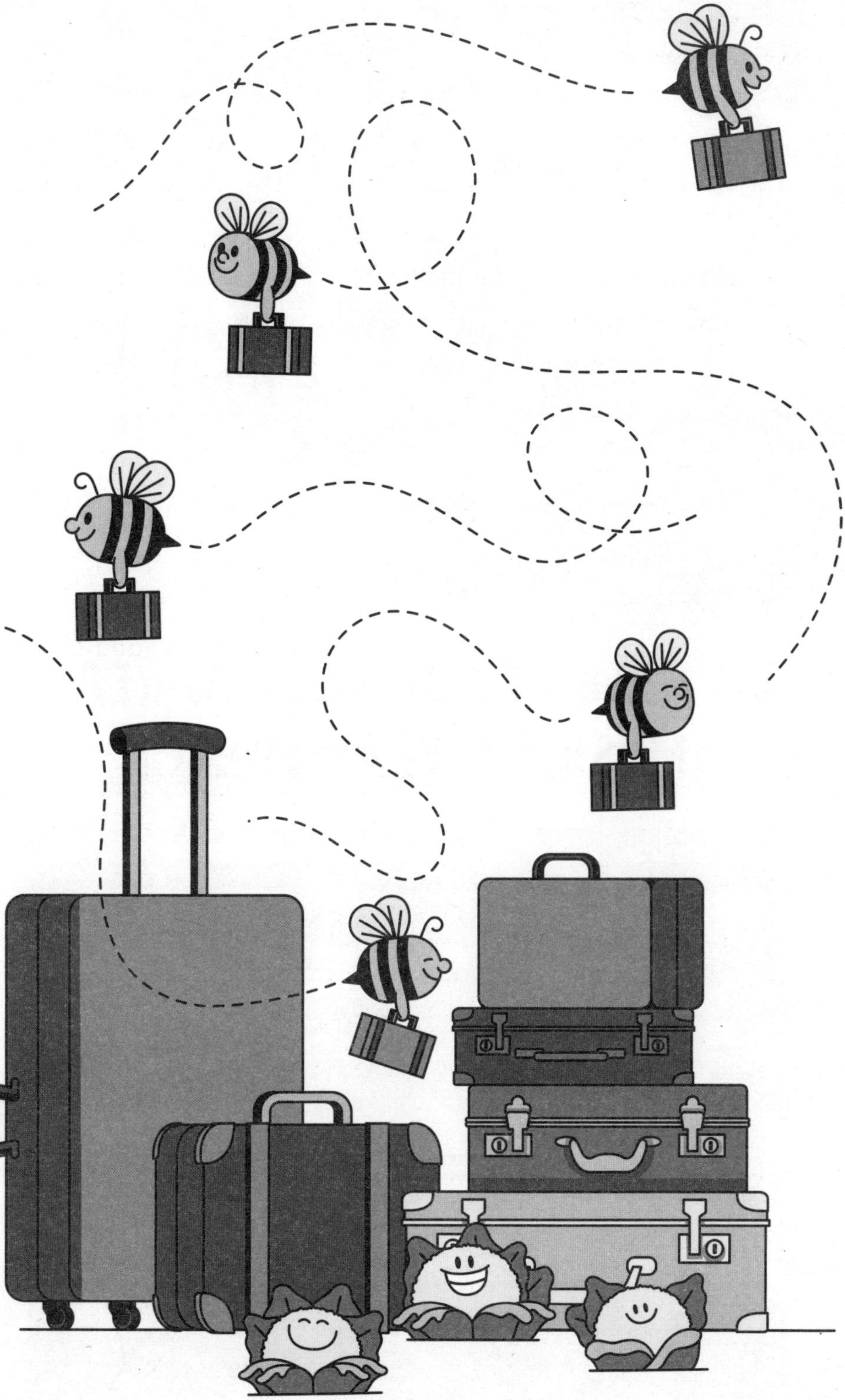

BAND CHAT

DO I NEED TO BE ABLE TO READ MUSIC TO PLAY MUSIC?

Alex: Hi there. Alex here. I've stayed out of this chapter for now because all this music-notation stuff seems very complicated. So here's a question: what do Paul McCartney, Taylor Swift and Jimi Hendrix have in common?

Band: They're all Sagittarians?

Alex: Good guess, but no. Paul McCartney is a Gemini. Do you give up?

Band: Sure.

Alex: Good. The answer is actually that, like me, all of them are unable to read music. So I'm as good at music as legendary record-breaking, award-winning singer-songwriter Paul McCartney. Bye!

Band: No you're not. But actually in some ways, annoyingly, you are.

Reading music is a useful tool but it is not essential to playing music. Apparently Jimi would use words and colours to express to his band how he wanted the music to be played.

When people don't read sheet music but are able to reproduce music they've heard, they have the ability to 'play by ear'. Music such as jazz and blues were traditionally passed down in this way.

So while reading and writing music is incredibly useful, it's not the only way to play. And it's definitely not the most fun bit about music!

ALEX HAS LEFT THE CONVERSATION.

WHAT DOES THE CONDUCTOR ACTUALLY DO?

The conductor is the person at the front of the orchestra who has sheet music and a little stick but no musical instrument. So what's the deal with conductors and written music?

The conductor makes sure all the musicians know what music to play and that they play it all together at the same time. When you have a large number of people all trying to do something together it can be very helpful to have one person for everyone to follow. So a conductor is a bit like a sports manager. You've probably watched a football match where the manager is screaming from the sidelines at the players to do something. Conducting is screaming with your arms, in front of a an **ENSEMBLE**, and every player has a ball and the ball is actually an instrument.

The conductor can direct musicians on everything from the tempo (speed) and time signature (how may beats there are in a bar) to the **DYNAMICS** (loud notes or soft notes). If everyone follows the conductor, then the music will sound rather lovely, like the musicians are playing as one.

It is important to remember that once the concert is over, the musicians must stop following the conductor. You should never follow a conductor back to their car or house, even if they accidentally wave their stick that way.

THE GRUESOME TALE OF JEAN-BAPTISTE LULLY

Long before conductors used batons (the conductor's wavy stick thing) they had a staff. Yes, like a wizard. A conductor was a wizard controlling an army of musicians. These musical wizards were not able to wave their staff in the air because it was far too heavy. Instead they pounded it on the floor, banging out the tempo of the piece so the orchestra would follow. And for a while this worked. That is until the enthusiastic French conductor Jean-Baptiste Lully (who also had a passion for dancing) came along.

Lully decided that he too should try this wizard-staff technique. 'Why not?' we hear you say. 'Pourquoi pas?' we almost hear the dead seventeenth-century composer say. Well, we'll answer both of you right now.

One night in 1687 Lully was conducting a performance of his composition *Te Deum* to celebrate the French King Louis XIV recovering from a surgery. In a particularly exciting part of the performance, Lully lifted the staff and, as he banged it down, he managed to strike his own foot with it. A gruesome condition called gangrene soon infected Lully's wounded limb. His doctors told him that he should have his leg amputated (chopped off) but Lully decided to take his chances with the infection. Maybe he thought someone might invent antibiotics in the next week or two.

Sadly for Lully that didn't happen until forty-two guinea pigs' lives later (in 1928, obviously) and he died shortly after the accident. Turns out Lully considered his love of dancing so great that he didn't want to lose a leg to the infection. Consequently he lost both legs, both arms, lungs, spleen, thumbs, bum, connective tissue... and you get the idea. Lully died.

MUSICAL TASKS

MUSICAL TASK NUMBER THREE

Sing a well-known song but only use a single note. At no point can you sing a higher or lower one than the note you start on.

Most interesting single-note song wins.

(This is particularly fun to do at Christmas. Pick any carol and sing it just on the one note. Soon you'll have your whole family singing merrily along.)

YOUR TIME STARTS NOW.

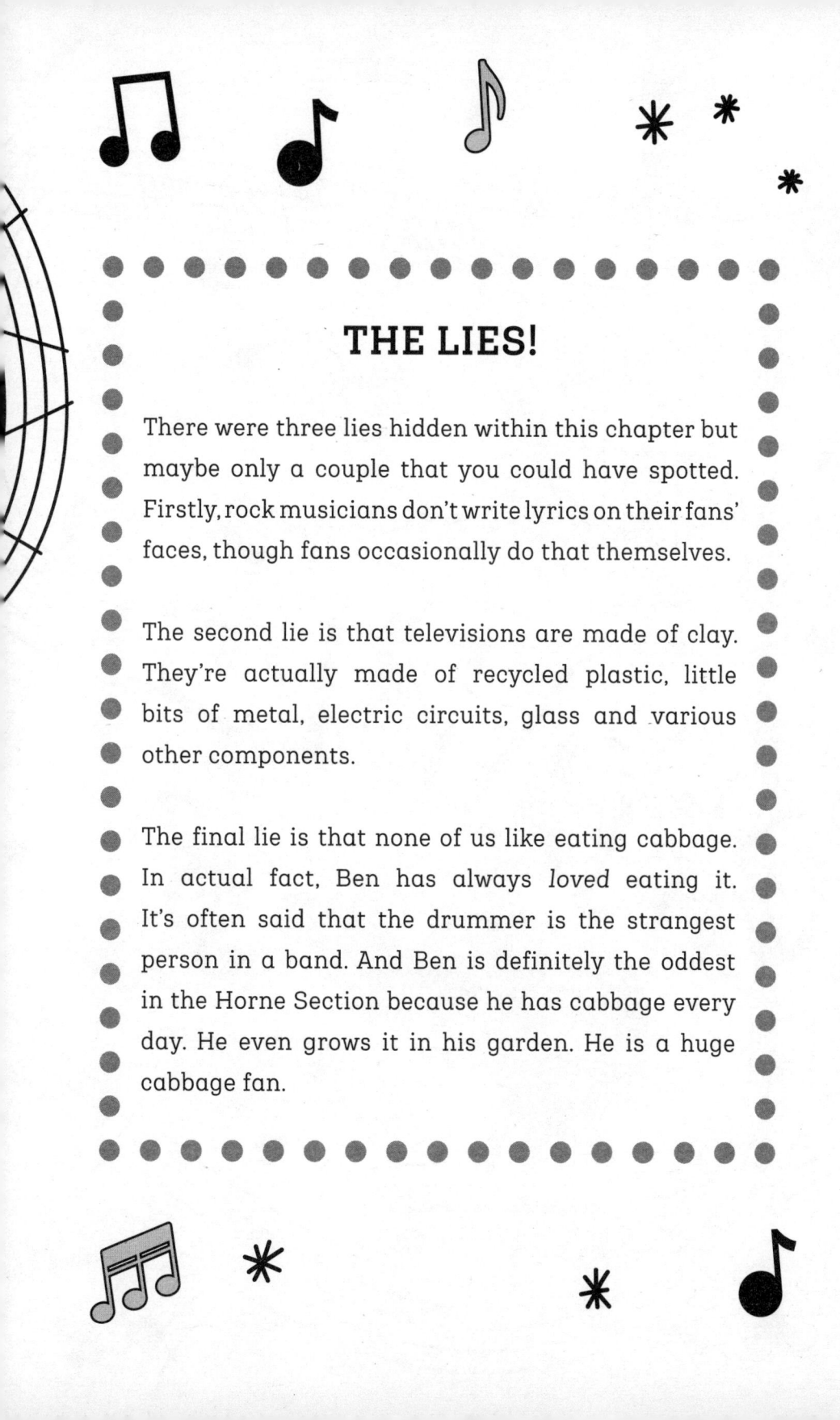

THE LIES!

There were three lies hidden within this chapter but maybe only a couple that you could have spotted. Firstly, rock musicians don't write lyrics on their fans' faces, though fans occasionally do that themselves.

The second lie is that televisions are made of clay. They're actually made of recycled plastic, little bits of metal, electric circuits, glass and various other components.

The final lie is that none of us like eating cabbage. In actual fact, Ben has always *loved* eating it. It's often said that the drummer is the strangest person in a band. And Ben is definitely the oddest in the Horne Section because he has cabbage every day. He even grows it in his garden. He is a huge cabbage fan.

CHAPTER

FOUR

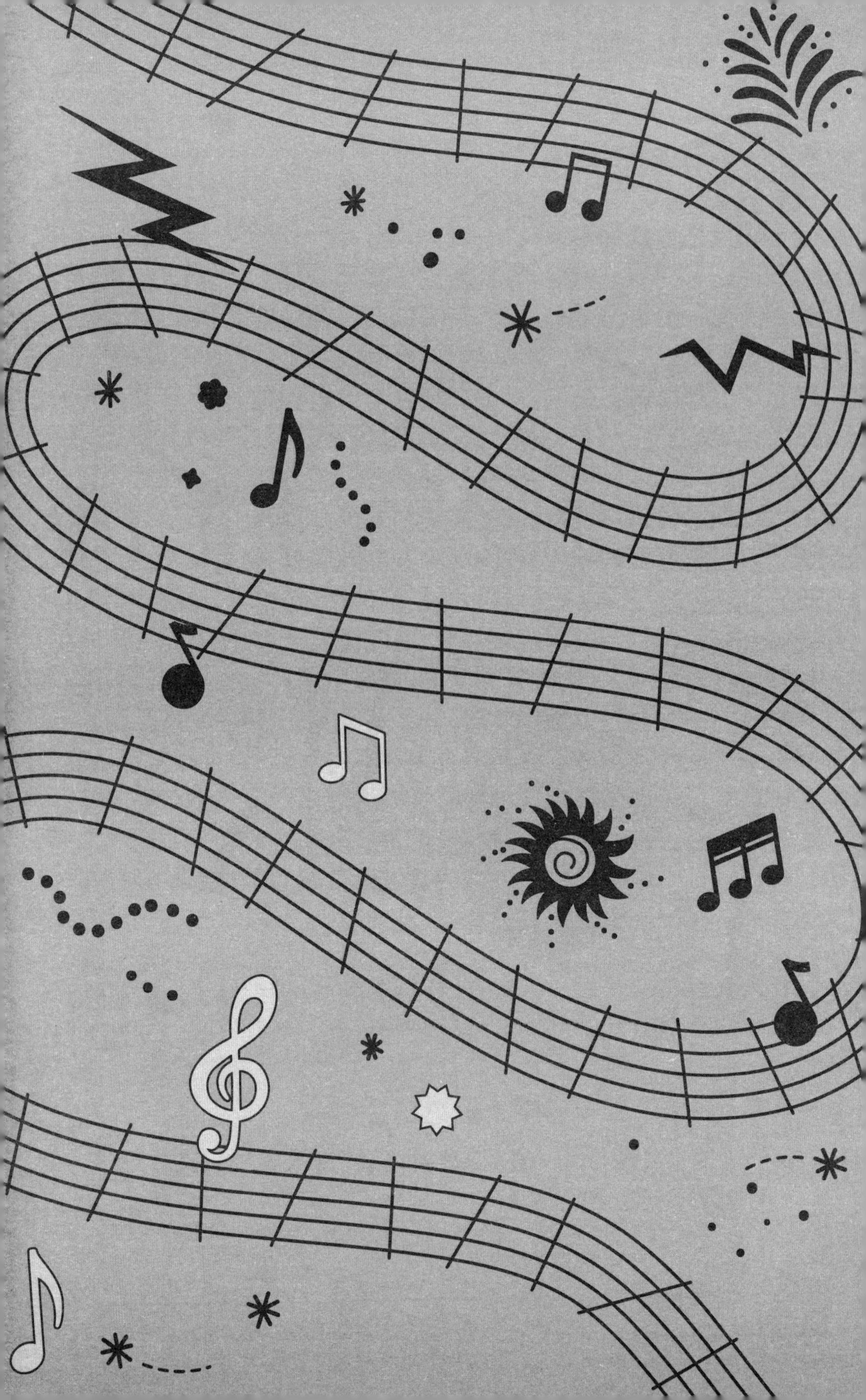

WHAT SORT OF MUSIC SHOULD I MAKE?

By now you've chosen an instrument (or two) - whether that's your voice, a drum kit, a flute, a hollowed-out cucumber or something else. You've learned how to read music (or not if it's not for you). And you've realized that I have a terrible lying habit. Apologies. Now I think it's about time you make some music.

But where to start? There are countless types of music (called genres), so how do you choose which one to play? Well, the band and I are here to help. We're going to describe the different genres so that you can explore them all before choosing. Think of us as a nice PE teacher who is going to show you every sport in the world, then let you pick which one you want to play. Also, you won't have to wear scratchy PE shorts or do any laps of a football pitch (unless you want to).

BAND CHAT

Alex: Hello, band, please can you tell us about all the different types of music?

Band: OK. We want you to start by imagining a time where there was nothing anywhere. A black emptiness before life began.

Alex: Sorry, are you talking to me?

Band: Sort of. You and the reader. Are you imagining a time before life began?

Alex: I'm trying but it's very difficult. I keep thinking about orange squash and shin pads and staplers and how much I dislike cabbage.

Band: Try harder.

Alex: OK, I'm now just thinking of an enormous nothingness. With one cabbage in the middle.

Band: OK, remove the cabbage. What can you hear?

Alex: Oh, it's very quiet.

Band: Exactly. There's no sound at all because NOTHING exists! Here we are at the beginning of time and guess what? The first thing that happens in the history of our universe is music, and it was probably the loudest and coolest music ever:

THE BIG BANG!

Band: OK, so it's not music as we traditionally understand it. But we know that music can have a very powerful effect on our lives and nothing could be more powerful than the creation of the universe. (Boring adults and clever scientists might argue that outer space is actually a vacuum and as a result there is no sound, but, despite what they say, it is called the BIG BANG! Not the 'big silent thing'.)

Alex: Right, this has all been nonsense so far. I'm going for a bath and when I come back I want you to be having a serious discussion about musical genres...

ALEX HAS LEFT THE CONVERSATION.

MUSICAL GENRES

JAZZ

This is the genre of music most of us in the band chose to study and play when we left school. What comes to mind when you hear the word 'jazz'? Is it berets and sunglasses? Is it musicians clicking their fingers while saying things like 'skwee-boppa-de-woo'? Is it music you have to listen to when you travel in a hotel lift or department store? Whichever it is, we believe jazz is one of the coolest genres of music going.

Some people, like us for example, say jazz was born in Louisiana, USA, in the mid-1800s. At that time in the city of New Orleans there was a huge population of enslaved African people. In fact, the governments of Britain, America and France (among others) profited from this terrible exploitation of people who led miserable lives working on farms performing back-breaking labour against their will and for no pay. Sometimes, however, they would come and play music in a spot called Congo Square. These gatherings brought together people from many different countries, which meant lots of unique sounds from each country were added to the mix.

Thanks to this combination of sounds and instruments, by 1900 a genre of jazz called ragtime became the most popular music of its era. It was played by guitarists, string bands, fiddlers, saxophonists and pianists and was a mixture of Cuban and Spanish-Caribbean rhythms, West African music, the blues and church music, blended with some **IMPROVISATION** and blue notes (which are notes BETWEEN normal notes, specific to jazz and blues music). Ragtime is really the first genre of jazz, and later ones were called Dixieland, swing, bebop, cool, freeform and fusion.

Are you a rebel? Do you like breaking rules? Then jazz could be the genre for you! Because in jazz you can make it up as you go along. It's a bit like football: as long as you know the basic rules, you can do what you want with the ball. You don't have to follow any definite instructions – just stay on the pitch and try to be brilliant.

When they play music, jazz bands leave gaps for the musicians to make melodies up that they think will sound excellent within the tune. So jazz musicians need to think on their feet (or bums if sitting at the piano or drums) and use their musical skills to express their endless creativity and react to what their band mates are playing. This is called improvisation and can produce the most amazing music, as well as some that is slightly difficult to listen to!

As we've got older we've learned that, with jazz, if you play anything with enough confidence then people will believe it's good. In fact, this attitude works across many things in life. If someone suggests you're playing jazz wrong, simply quote the wise words of American jazz trumpeter and singer Louis Armstrong:

> If you have to ask what jazz is, you'll never know.

Jazz can be played in lots of different ways, which certainly keeps things interesting. Sometimes entire jazz albums are created using a single instrument, usually a guitar or piano or keyboard. Have a listen to Charles Mingus's *Mingus Plays Piano* or Thelonious Monk's *Solo Monk*, both of which are full albums created by American jazz artists using only piano.

There are also lots of jazz albums with any number of musicians playing together, including something called 'big band' (different to the Big Bang). A big band is typically made up of around seventeen musicians, including the rhythm section (guitar, piano, bass and drums) and then a combination of other wind and brass instruments. To help you imagine this particular type of music, here's a picture of a big band in a Mini car:

The number of musicians and types of instruments involved in jazz music can change depending on the music being played. So if you currently play classical bassoon but love jazz, then don't give up hope; there is probably a band out there just waiting to discover a jazzy bassoonist!

This is all great, but what does jazz actually sound like?

OK. That's a tricky question. We'll do our best. Do you know the song 'When the Saints Go Marching In'? Good. Well, let's try to make that sound jazzy. First let's sing:

OH WHEN THE SAINTS

GO MARCHING IN

OH WHEN THE SAINTS GO MARCHING IN.

Well done if you sang that nice and loudly. But now let's add a bit of jazz improvising in between the lines. Even louder this time:

OH WHEN THE SAINTS

DOO-BA-DOO-BA-DOO-BA-DOOOOO!

GO MARCHING IN

SKA-BA-DIDDLY-DOO-BA-DOOOO!

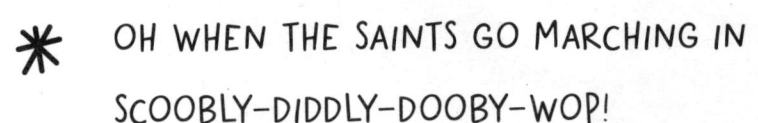

OH WHEN THE SAINTS GO MARCHING IN

SCOOBLY-DIDDLY-DOOBY-WOP!

That was too loud actually. But congratulations – that was nearly jazz music!

Before we move on here are some jazz tracks and albums you should listen to. (We'll give you some suggestions for every genre in this chapter, so you can dip your ear into all kinds of different sounds. After all, it's one thing describing music but it's usually better to actually hear it.)

YOUR FIRST JAZZ PLAYLIST

SCOTT JOPLIN
'MAPLE LEAF RAG' (1899)

LOUIS ARMSTRONG
'OH WHEN THE SAINTS' (1938)

MILES DAVIS
'SO WHAT' (1958)

ELLA FITZGERALD
'OLD MCDONALD' (1966)

WEATHER REPORT
'BIRDLAND' (1977)

EZRA COLLECTIVE
FEAT. KOJEY RADICAL
'NO CONFUSION' (2022)

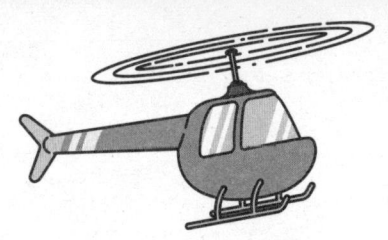

CLASSICAL

Now let's look at the music your parents pretend to like. Western classical music has been around for a really, really long time. Ages. At least 1,500 years, so that's an awful lot of music to listen to in your spare time. There's a huge number of different types of music that all come under the label of classical. Gregorian chanting is religious singing, usually in Latin, that people used to do in the Catholic church in the seventh to tenth centuries. Or there's the more recent Karlheinz Stockhausen's *Helicopter String Quartet*, which involves four musicians playing music in four separate helicopters.

> I always thought Gregorian chanting was just people called Greg or Ian shouting at a rugby match.

If more classical music involved aircraft, it might be more popular with young people, but unfortunately as this piece is so tricky to perform it is very rarely played. Each of the four helicopters needs a pilot, a sound technician, a television transmitter, lots more fiddly equipment, a huge performance space with four columns of TVs and loudspeakers, a sound projectionist with a special mixing desk, as well as the four string musicians themselves. It is not how classical music normally works!

Classical music is usually split up into the following time periods:

MEDIEVAL MUSIC (500–1400)

RENAISSANCE MUSIC (1400–1600)

BAROQUE MUSIC (1600–1750)

CLASSICAL MUSIC (1750–1830)

ROMANTIC MUSIC (1830–1920)

TWENTIETH AND TWENTY-FIRST CENTURY MUSIC (1920–NOW!)

500–1400
MEDIEVAL MUSIC

During this period music was primarily used to worship God, with songs like those Gregorian chants we mentioned earlier. Music was mainly sung during this time, but there were also some instruments used, such as the lyra, which was an early type of violin but shaped like a pear. Honestly! Don't believe me? Don't call me a lyra. Also the lute, which was an early version of the guitar, the dulcimer, a kind of box with strings stretched over it that you hit with spoon-shaped mallets (sounds fun) and early versions of trumpets and some percussion instruments.

1400–1600
RENAISSANCE MUSIC

The Renaissance was a period in European history when big scientific discoveries were made and great art was produced. At this time art became more sophisticated and people were becoming more educated. Reading music became more widespread and music was in high demand, both at home (with newly printed music) and at public concerts. The music had become more emotional too. Singing was still most common, but instrumental music was also being written for small groups of musicians.

The crumhorn was a popular instrument of this period. Players would blow in one end and put their fingers over holes, which ran along the length of the pipe, to change the note. A bit like a recorder except, rather than being straight, it was shaped like the letter 'J' to direct the sound back to the person playing it. So more like a musical boomerang. Other instruments included the harpsichord (a bit like a piano) and the organ (a lot like an organ).

> That is a great name. I wonder if Alex Horne's great grandmother was called Crum Horne.

1600–1750
BAROQUE MUSIC

The word Baroque comes from the Portuguese 'barroco' which means 'a pearl with a non-spherical shape'. This does not help us at all with understanding what sort of music it is.

Forgetting about non-spherical pearls, Baroque music is often elaborate and emotional, unlike the more stuffy music that came before. Because it was a bit more interesting, the Catholic church encouraged use of the style to try to appeal to more people. Baroque was normally written for small groups of musicians, usually using harpsichords or organs rather than brass or wind instruments. Musical pieces called **CONCERTOS** and **SONATAS** were also written for a solo instrumentalist, so they could show off their flamboyant techniques.

This was also when composers started writing opera, which is a long, dramatic composition telling an entire story, sung with instrumental backing. (Like an episode of *EastEnders* but set to music.) Operas were and still are big, extravagant events.

Some notable composers from the Baroque period were J. S. Bach (from Germany), Vivaldi (from Italy) and Handel (from Germany), none of whom were spheres and all of whom could be described as pearls, so maybe it's not such a bad description after all.

BACH

HANDEL

VIVALDI

1750–1830
CLASSICAL MUSIC

Music in the Classical era had bigger orchestras that played long musical pieces called **SYMPHONIES**. New, rich-sounding melodic instruments, such as the clarinet, oboe, flute, horns and trumpet, were now a part of the orchestra, bringing a much more varied and energetic sound.

Some of the most famous composers came from the Classical era. Wolfgang Amadeus Mozart, for example, was a child genius born in Austria. He wrote his first composition when he was just five years old, and he ended up writing over 600 works in his lifetime, many of which you'll probably have heard before.

Beethoven, who was born in Germany, was another famous Classical composer, and he wrote nine symphonies. This is not as many as Mozart (who wrote 41), but people *really* like Beethoven's ones. Another notable Austrian composer was Joseph Haydn – he was a bit overshadowed by Beethoven and Mozart because he was usually busy playing Haydn seek.

1830–1920
ROMANTIC MUSIC

Music in the Romantic era was much more dramatic and emotional. Composers started to write longer, more complicated pieces and orchestras became even bigger, now featuring new instruments like drums, tuned percussion, harps, double bass, clarinet and many more.

1920–NOW
TWENTIETH AND TWENTY-FIRST CENTURY MUSIC

In the twentieth century the world had become more interconnected. Classical music started to take influences from countries across the globe, moving it in all kinds of new directions. Because of this, twentieth-century music can't really be described in one way, as it is made up of so many different composers with their own unique style, including French musicians Debussy and Satie, Austrian-American Schoenberg, Stravinsky from Russia, Elgar from England, and many more.

Twentieth-century classical music is also made up of many different styles including influences from folk and jazz. These varieties (also called subgenres) include romanticism, expressionism, neoclassicism, serialism, atonality, electronic, experimental and minimalism which really are complicated words for what is meant to be fun.

Recording technology also changed the way classical music was listened to. Previously people might only ever hear the great classical pieces once in their lives, probably at a performance, whereas now people could listen over and over on their record players at home.

CLASSIC SKILLS

Playing classical music requires incredible skill with an instrument, and as the genre developed, composers came up with very sophisticated and complicated pieces of music. For example, one of the most famous classical composers was a German man called Johann Sebastian Bach, who was born in 1685 (you might remember his name from the Baroque era). One of his pieces, called a fugue, is written for the harpsichord and it contains not one, not two, not a hundred, not three but FIVE different melodies that are all meant to be played at once. Bearing in mind the number of fingers we have, you can imagine that's not an easy piece to play.

There's another very famous piece of music called 'Flight of the Bumblebee', which was written by the Russian composer Nikolai Rimsky-Korsakov in 1900. The fast tempo makes this piece of music sound a lot like a bumblebee flying randomly around your kitchen. That's the idea anyway, and it's a famously difficult tune to play.

THE COMPOSERS OF CLASSICAL MUSIC ARE OFTEN MORE FAMOUS THAN THE PEOPLE PLAYING IT. SO IF, AFTER STUDYING FOR YEARS, YOU STILL CAN'T PLAY 'TWINKLE, TWINKLE, LITTLE STAR' ON THE KEYBOARD, THEN THERE IS HOPE. YOU COULD START COMPOSING MUSIC INSTEAD, AND STILL END UP BECOMING A WORLD-FAMOUS ARTIST WITHOUT ANY OF THAT BORING PRACTICE.

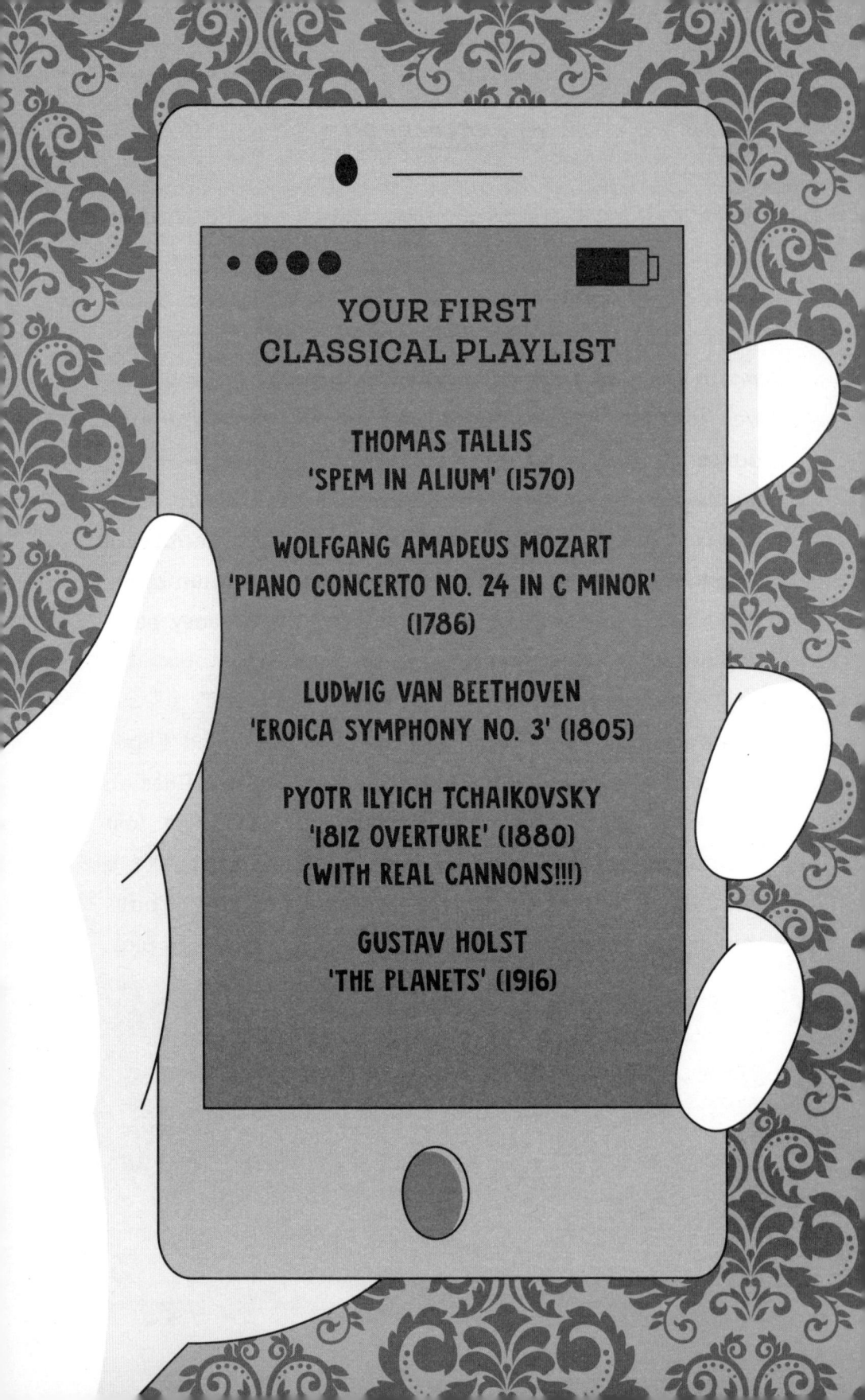

YOUR FIRST CLASSICAL PLAYLIST

THOMAS TALLIS
'SPEM IN ALIUM' (1570)

WOLFGANG AMADEUS MOZART
'PIANO CONCERTO NO. 24 IN C MINOR'
(1786)

LUDWIG VAN BEETHOVEN
'EROICA SYMPHONY NO. 3' (1805)

PYOTR ILYICH TCHAIKOVSKY
'1812 OVERTURE' (1880)
(WITH REAL CANNONS!!!)

GUSTAV HOLST
'THE PLANETS' (1916)

POP

Pop is short for popular music and, despite its name, it is the most boring genre of music.

As the name suggests, pop music is a word to describe music that lots of people enjoy. Some people consider the jazz music of the 1920s and 1930s to be the first pop music. Others consider rock 'n' roll in the 1950s to be the first genuine pop music. Whichever side of the argument you're on, most people do agree on how this genre of music became so popular and such a big part of everyday life. It started in the early 1920s, when electronic recording equipment was invented. Jazz records were made and played on the radio or, if you were rich, at home on your record player. (A record player cost about the same as a car back then.) More and more people heard jazz and liked it!

> I just want to apologize on behalf of the band. They are jazz musicians, which means they're very jealous of pop musicians, because most pop musicians are more successful than them. So remember that the next few paragraphs are written by people who actually wish they'd spent their lives learning popular music rather than unpopular music.

Over the next twenty years rock 'n' roll emerged and became even more popular. At the same time technology was developing and becoming more widespread. Radios were everywhere at this point, and jukeboxes started popping up in pubs and cafes, meaning people could choose which records to listen and dance to when they were out and about. And most people chose to listen to American singer Elvis Presley. Elvis is still the most successful solo pop artist of all time, having sold more than one billion records so far!

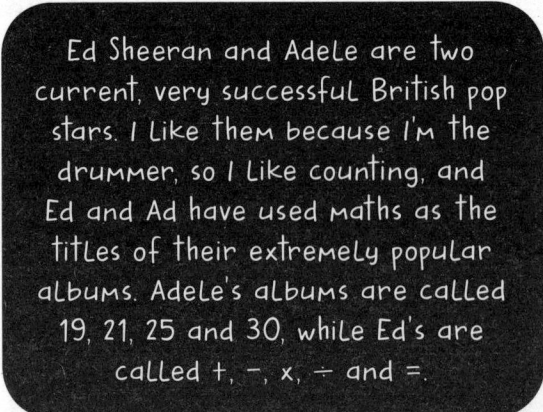

> Ed Sheeran and Adele are two current, very successful British pop stars. I like them because I'm the drummer, so I like counting, and Ed and Ad have used maths as the titles of their extremely popular albums. Adele's albums are called 19, 21, 25 and 30, while Ed's are called +, −, x, ÷ and =.

> Adele also features on an album called *1988*, so if you want to know the true meaning of their music, you can just combine them like this: 19 + 21 − 25 x 30 ÷ 1988, which gives you the very satisfying answer of 39.622736418511066, which just happens to be my lucky number.

Pop is by far the most likely genre to make you rich beyond your wildest dreams. Today's top-selling artist is Rihanna with 250 million sales to date. Although in 2016 her album was beaten in sales by Mozart when a 200-disc boxset of his music was released to honour the 225th anniversary of his death.

The clever thing about pop music is that it takes parts of nearly all the other genres but removes the tricky bits. The power and heaviness of rock music is toned down to a level that your parents might find agreeable (have a listen to the American rock band Bon Jovi to see what we mean). And the wildness of jazz, with all its dizzying improvisations and out-of-time cymbal crashes, is turned into a smooth groovy hit that is the perfect background accompaniment for any occasion (have a listen to the English funk band Jamiroquai and you'll see what we mean).

And if folk lyrics are a little too sad, pop songs simplify the twiddly music and turn the lyrics into a song about love (try British folk band Mumford & Sons and you'll get the idea).

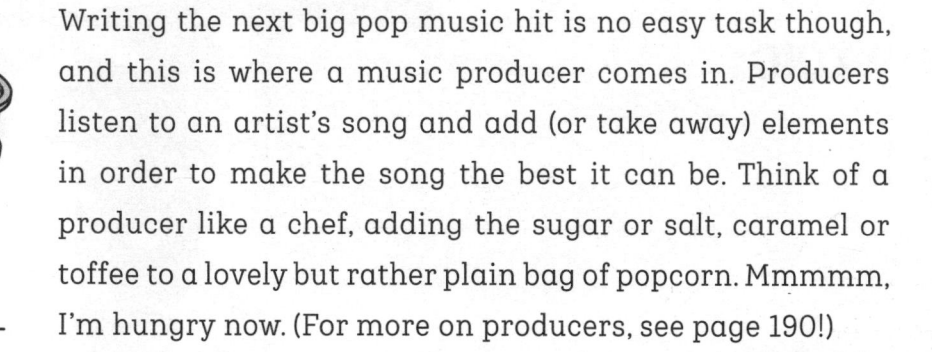

Writing the next big pop music hit is no easy task though, and this is where a music producer comes in. Producers listen to an artist's song and add (or take away) elements in order to make the song the best it can be. Think of a producer like a chef, adding the sugar or salt, caramel or toffee to a lovely but rather plain bag of popcorn. Mmmmm, I'm hungry now. (For more on producers, see page 190!)

Here's a list of the first and second bestselling pop artists of each decade:

1950s
1 > Elvis Presley **2 >** Frank Sinatra

1960s
1 > The Beatles **2 >** Elvis Presley

1970s
1 > Elton John **2 >** The Rolling Stones

1980s
1 > Prince **2 >** Madonna

1990s
1 > Mariah Carey **2 >** Madonna

2000s
1 > Eminem **2 >** Madonna

2010s
1 > Adele **2 >** Drake

YOUR FIRST POP PLAYLIST

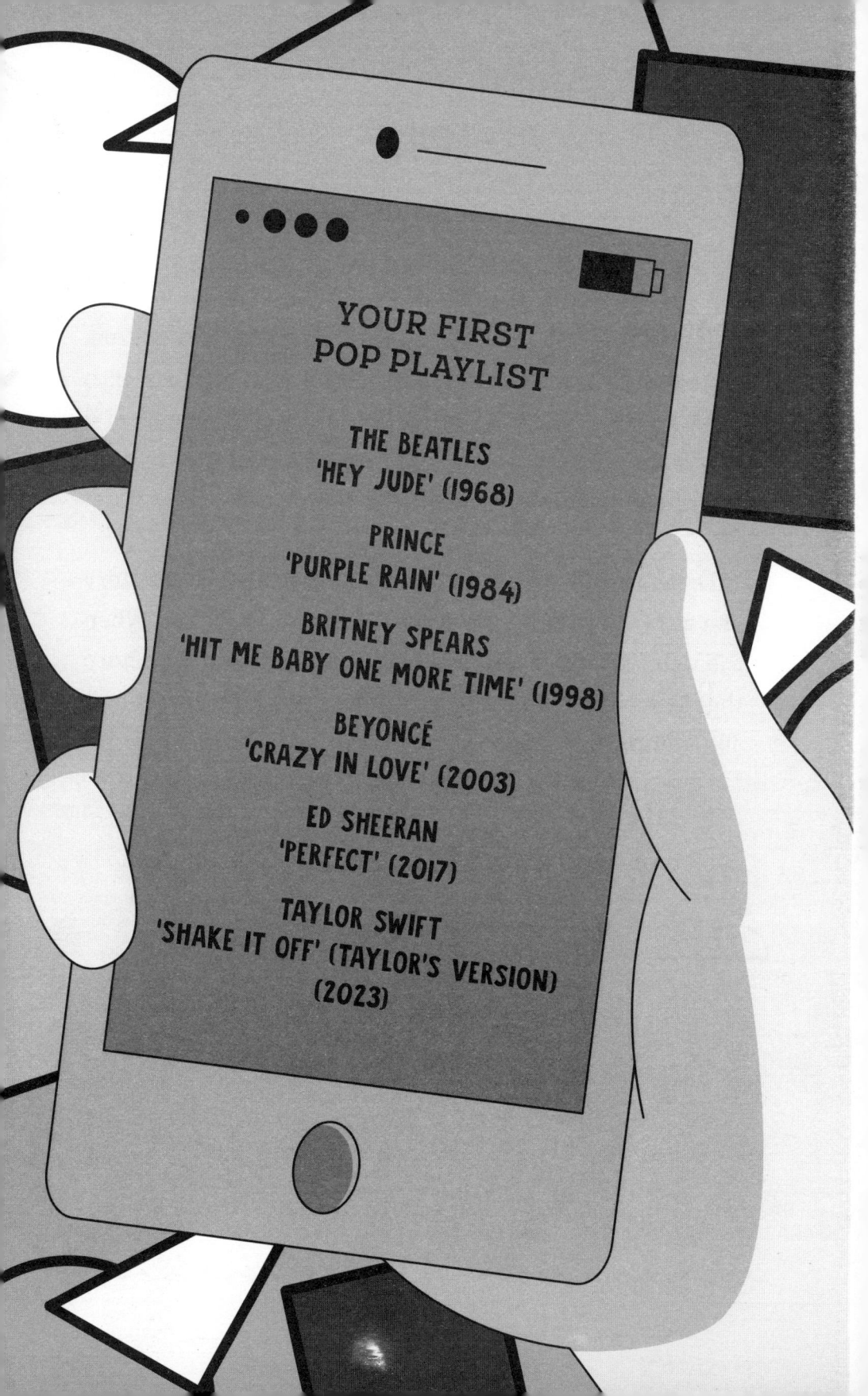

THE BEATLES
'HEY JUDE' (1968)

PRINCE
'PURPLE RAIN' (1984)

BRITNEY SPEARS
'HIT ME BABY ONE MORE TIME' (1998)

BEYONCÉ
'CRAZY IN LOVE' (2003)

ED SHEERAN
'PERFECT' (2017)

TAYLOR SWIFT
'SHAKE IT OFF' (TAYLOR'S VERSION) (2023)

FOLK

Are you into magic and ghosts? Do you want to go to parties in the woods? Then folk music might be the genre for you!

Traditionally folk music was a musical history lesson, played on instruments that had been around for ages, with lyrics all about the cultures, beliefs, tales and legends of a particular country. These songs would explore quite dark and often miserable themes.

Take the old folk tune 'The Twa Sisters', which tells the story of a girl killing her sister by pushing her into the sea. When the sister's body is found it has turned into a magic harp that sings a song to the village, telling the truth about how she was killed by her own sister!

'The Cruel Mother' tells the story of a mum who kills her sons, then comes home to see two boys. 'They're not mine,' she says, 'otherwise they would be dressed far more smartly.' The boys reveal themselves to be the ghosts of her murdered children and remind her that not only did she not dress them smartly, she did, in fact, kill them and bury them in the woods. A cruel mother indeed!

Folk music is still very popular today. Old folk tunes continue to be passed down through the generations and played at family gatherings as well as concerts and festivals all over the world. And modern folk music, which combines traditional folk styles with other genres like rock 'n' roll, is still being written and performed by bands and musicians like American singer-songwriter Bob Dylan and British singer-songwriter Laura Marling.

One of the more fun things about folk music is the traditional instruments that are used, which we don't often see in pop or classical music. As a folk musician you could toot on an ocarina, which is a small sweet-sounding wind instrument that looks like a seashell. Or try a Celtic harp, which is nice and soft and beautiful sounding. Or perhaps you'd like to play a kulintang, which is a tuned set of gongs from south-east Asia that sounds beautiful and is also very, very loud.

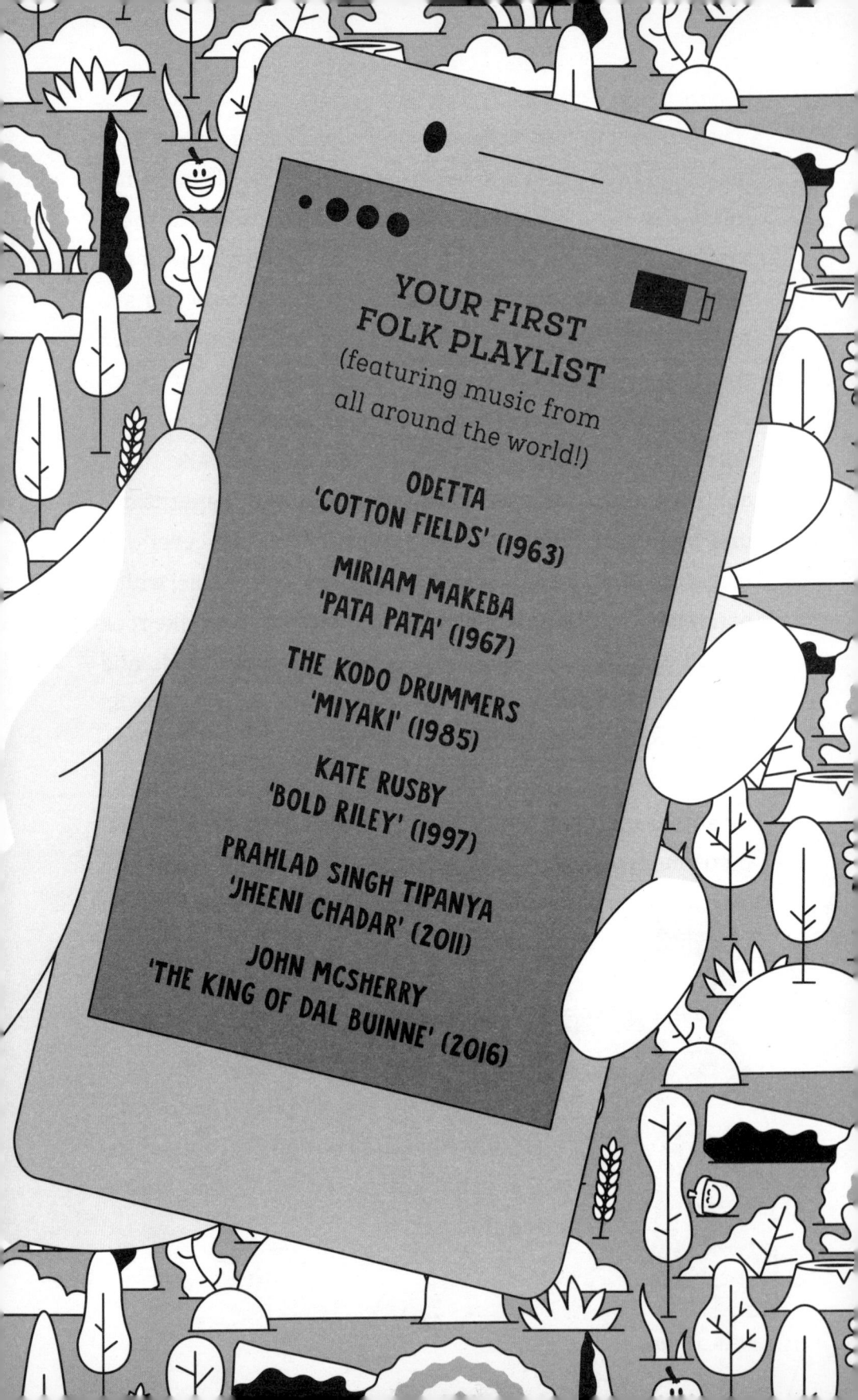

YOUR FIRST FOLK PLAYLIST
(featuring music from all around the world!)

ODETTA
'COTTON FIELDS' (1963)

MIRIAM MAKEBA
'PATA PATA' (1967)

THE KODO DRUMMERS
'MIYAKI' (1985)

KATE RUSBY
'BOLD RILEY' (1997)

PRAHLAD SINGH TIPANYA
'JHEENI CHADAR' (2011)

JOHN MCSHERRY
'THE KING OF DAL BUINNE' (2016)

REGGAE

Imagine a picturesque tropical island where the sun shines all year and a warm turquoise sea laps at beautiful white-sand beaches. Now imagine the music that would come from such a place and you will magically start to hear the wonderful sounds of reggae, a musical genre that originated in the late 1960s on the island of Jamaica. The catchy rhythms soon raced around the world and reggae is a hugely popular style of music today.

The lyrics of reggae songs often discuss current events, politics or religion. Bob Marley is undoubtedly the most famous reggae artist and some of his most popular songs have important messages. He wrote 'Get Up, Stand Up' after visiting the island of Haiti and seeing the poverty there, and 'I Shot the Sheriff' is all about police and violence. But reggae isn't all serious – you'll still find lots of songs about love and partying. For instance, Bob Marley's song 'Three Little Birds' is literally about three little birds!

To get slightly more technical, the music itself is unique for a couple of reasons. The bass guitar plays a very important role in reggae and it has a lot more to do in this genre compared to many others. Normally bassists are expected to play the basic notes in a song and keep time with the drummer, but the bass player in a reggae band has a bit more freedom, meaning the music sounds nice and loose and melodic.

Another reason reggae music is unique is something called the skank! The skank is when one, or a few, of the instruments emphasize the second and fourth beats (the 'offbeats') of each bar. This makes such a strong rhythm that it's almost impossible not to bob up and down on those beats when listening to reggae music. Try it right now! Listen to one of the tracks on our reggae playlist and see how long you can sit still for.

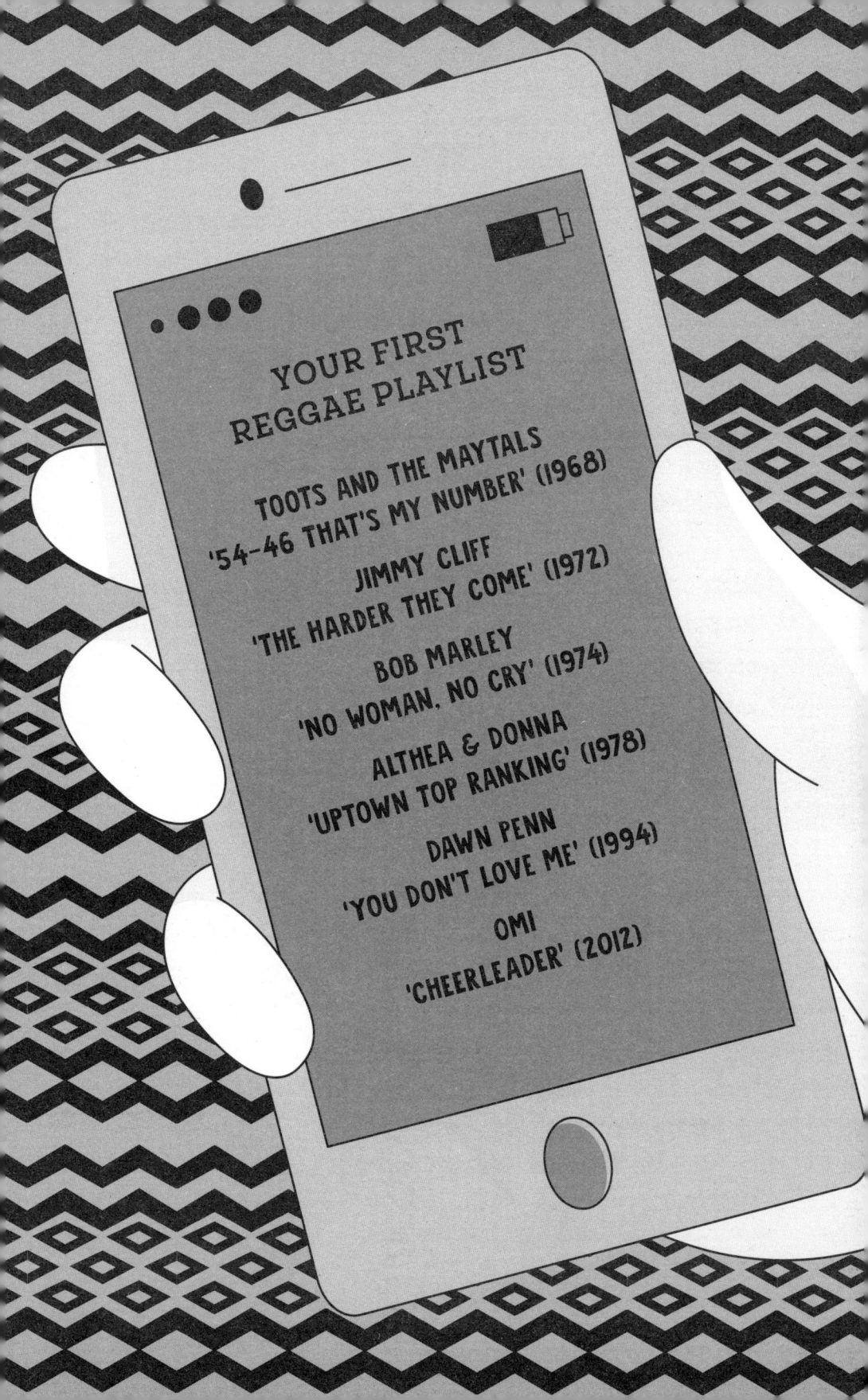

YOUR FIRST REGGAE PLAYLIST

TOOTS AND THE MAYTALS
'54-46 THAT'S MY NUMBER' (1968)

JIMMY CLIFF
'THE HARDER THEY COME' (1972)

BOB MARLEY
'NO WOMAN, NO CRY' (1974)

ALTHEA & DONNA
'UPTOWN TOP RANKING' (1978)

DAWN PENN
'YOU DON'T LOVE ME' (1994)

OMI
'CHEERLEADER' (2012)

ROCK

We've said it a couple of times now: the electric guitar is the coolest of all the instruments. You look cool holding it, it looks cool hanging on your wall and it's especially cool when you're using it to smash up the rest of your band mates' instruments during a gig (more on that later). And the electric guitar is probably the most important instrument in rock (a word that you should really shout while holding up your fist with the little finger and thumb pointing out).

Rock 'n' roll (to give it its full name) was born in the late 1940s in America and it has since had many musical babies of its own, such as progressive rock, adult-orientated rock, Christian rock, electronic rock and medieval rock.

Basically think of any word, put it before the word 'rock', and there'll be a band somewhere playing that sort of music.

As with reggae, rock music has often been about rebellion, going against what everyone else is saying or doing, and criticizing those in power. If you want to dip your toe into this sort of thing, there's a huge English band called Black Sabbath who are often credited with inventing heavy metal music. They've sold over 70 million records, including the song 'War Pigs', which they wrote as a way to protest against the Vietnam War. Or you could listen to Frank Zappa, a genius American guitarist and songwriter, who wrote about racism in his song 'Trouble Every Day'.

Such an expressive and high-energy genre can also result in some wild antics on stage. In 1967, Jimi Hendrix was due to perform at the Monterey Pop Festival in the USA. This was his big homecoming gig after a year winning over audiences in Europe, and Jimi saw it as an opportunity to announce himself on home soil, where he was still relatively unknown. He was performing after a band called The Who. They had destroyed the stage and set off smoke bombs, and Jimi had to upstage them. So at the end of his last song, called 'Fire', he set his guitar alight! You definitely shouldn't do this at home. (Or school. Or anywhere) but his risky plan worked a treat as he became the talking point of the festival and was soon viewed as the hottest guitarist on the planet. The blackened remains of the guitar were later sold for $380,000!

A few years later, in 1967, The Who's drummer took the tradition a step further by blowing up his drums at the end of a TV performance! It could have been the end of a great rock band but luckily nobody was badly hurt. Many bands have continued the tradition of destroying their instruments at the end of a show, from Jimi Hendrix to Matt Bellamy (lead singer of the English rock band Muse). In fact, Matt holds the record for number of guitars smashed while on tour – a whopping 140!

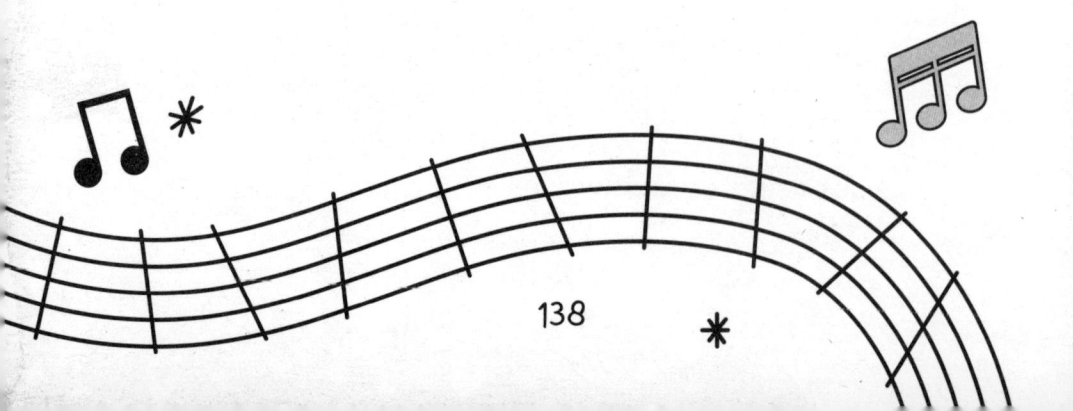

YOUR FIRST ROCK PLAYLIST

LED ZEPPELIN
'WHOLE LOTTA LOVE' (1969)

THE RAMONES
'BLITZKRIEG BOP' (1976)

JOAN JETT & THE BLACKHEARTS
'I LOVE ROCK 'N' ROLL' (1981)

NIRVANA
'SMELLS LIKE TEEN SPIRIT' (1991)

THE WHITE STRIPES
'SEVEN NATION ARMY' (2003)

WET LEG
'CHAISE LONGUE' (2022)

HIP HOP

Hip hop is a style of music but it's also a cultural movement that originated in Black communities in New York in the 1970s. This means that, through hip hop music, all sorts of things changed. It wasn't just the music itself that grew but things like art (with the growth of graffiti) and dance (with styles like body popping).

The music began at parties! DJs would use two record players at once and scratch records back and forth to create new sounds. For example, they would play part of the record (often a drum fill) for a short period of time. Then they would pull the record back to the beginning of the drum fill so that it played again, then again and again, so you would get a very short section of the original song repeated over and over on a 'loop'.

This technique was invented by a DJ called Grandma Flush. Sorry, no, not Grandma Flush. GRANDMASTER FLASH! Grandmaster Flash stuck bits of Sellotape on his records to remind him where his favourite drum fills were in the song.

Then along came the invention of drum machines. A drum machine is an electronic musical instrument that can make percussion sounds and drum beats. This meant hip hop artists were able to create their own beats rather than relying on samples from records.

But what is a sample? I hear you ask.

Sampling – still very popular in hip hop today – is a technique where a musician takes a section of a song (the 'sample') that already exists and uses that section, sometimes looped, in a different way to create a new song.

The first big mainstream hip hop hit was 'Rapper's Delight' by American band the Sugarhill Gang and it featured a sample of the song 'Good Times' by another American band called Chic.

Talking of rappers, the **VOCAL** style of rapping is another important feature of hip hop music. Rapping is all about talking and rhyming lyrics to the beat of a piece of music in a very rhythmic way. Sometimes people say that the word 'rap' comes from the first letters of 'Rhythm And Poetry'; but others say that that's just a happy coincidence. Maybe it stands for 'Raspberries And Pears'. Or… 'REALLY ANGRY PYJAMAS'!

Rappers are sometimes called MCs. 'MC' is short for 'master of ceremonies'. Rappers tend to have fun names such as Missy Elliot, André 3000, Big Daddy Kane and Little Alex Horne.

Eminem is a rapper who, like a lot of his fellow hip hop artists, has several different names – including Slim Shady, Evil, M&M, MC Double M or Marshall Mathers III (which is what his parents called him).

> My real name is Alex James Jeffery Horne, but people also call me Shakey, Al, Little Alex Horne, the Musical Maestro, the most important one in the Horne Section or just the man with the beard and the stick.

SEE IF YOU CAN MATCH THESE OTHER RAPPERS WITH THEIR REAL NAMES:

Cardi B	Belcalis Almánzar
Jay-Z	Antwan Patton
Drake	Christopher Brian Bridges
Ludacris	Cheryl James and Sandra Denton
Little Simz	
Queen Latifah	Dana Elaine Owens
50 Cent	Curtis Jackson III
The Notorious B.I.G.	Christopher Wallace
Lil Wayne	Dwayne Carter Jr
Missy Elliot	Aubrey Graham
	Simbiatu Abisola Abiola Ajikawo
Salt-N-Pepa	Amala Ratna Zandile Dlamini
Doja Cat	Shawn Carter
Big Boi	Melissa Arnette Elliott

You can find the answers on page 274.

Eminem also holds the Guinness World Record for most words rapped in a song and the fastest rap in a song. In one track, he fits 225 words into a 30 second section. This means he averages 7.5 words every second!

> I say, I say, I say, that is a very fast way to sing songs.

Willip's sentence there has fifteen words. Try saying that in TWO SECONDS! And then try saying the same sentence fifteen times in half a minute. If you can do it, you've got yourself a world record, my friend.

RAP FACT:

WILLIAM SHAKESPEARE INVENTED RAP MUSIC. HIS EARLY PLAYS AND POEMS WERE PERFORMED BY THE FIRST RAP ARTISTS WHO WOULD 'SPIT' HIS WORDS OVER THE TOP OF MUSICIANS PLAYING LUTES, VIOLS, DRUMS AND PIPES.

YOUR FIRST HIP HOP PLAYLIST

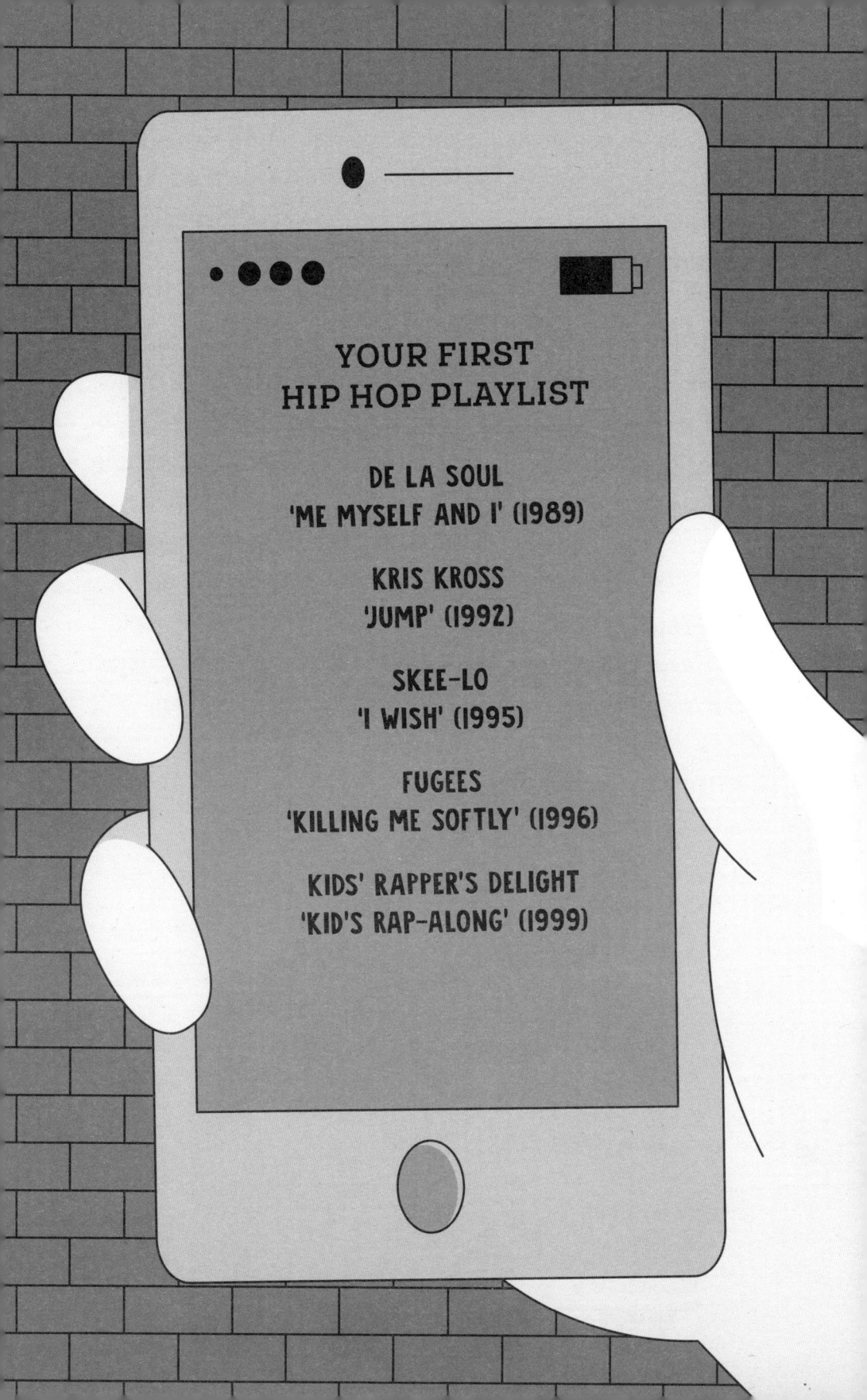

DE LA SOUL
'ME MYSELF AND I' (1989)

KRIS KROSS
'JUMP' (1992)

SKEE-LO
'I WISH' (1995)

FUGEES
'KILLING ME SOFTLY' (1996)

KIDS' RAPPER'S DELIGHT
'KID'S RAP-ALONG' (1999)

So there we go. There are loads of different musical genres for you to listen to. Try them all, listen to our playlist suggestions and see which ones you like best. Then you can decide which type of music you want to play!

Just like buying something from an ice-cream van, we recommend trying everything once before you decide. You may well like lots of different musical flavours or all of them! You don't need to limit yourself to one thing. Ed Sheeran plays pop, folk and rock, Taylor Swift is known for her pop, country and folk music, while Beyoncé can turn her hand (which she does brilliantly) to R&B, pop, hip hop, country and dance. We haven't had time to explore all those sounds here, but there is a whole world of musical genres out there just waiting for you to listen to them.

MUSICAL TASKS

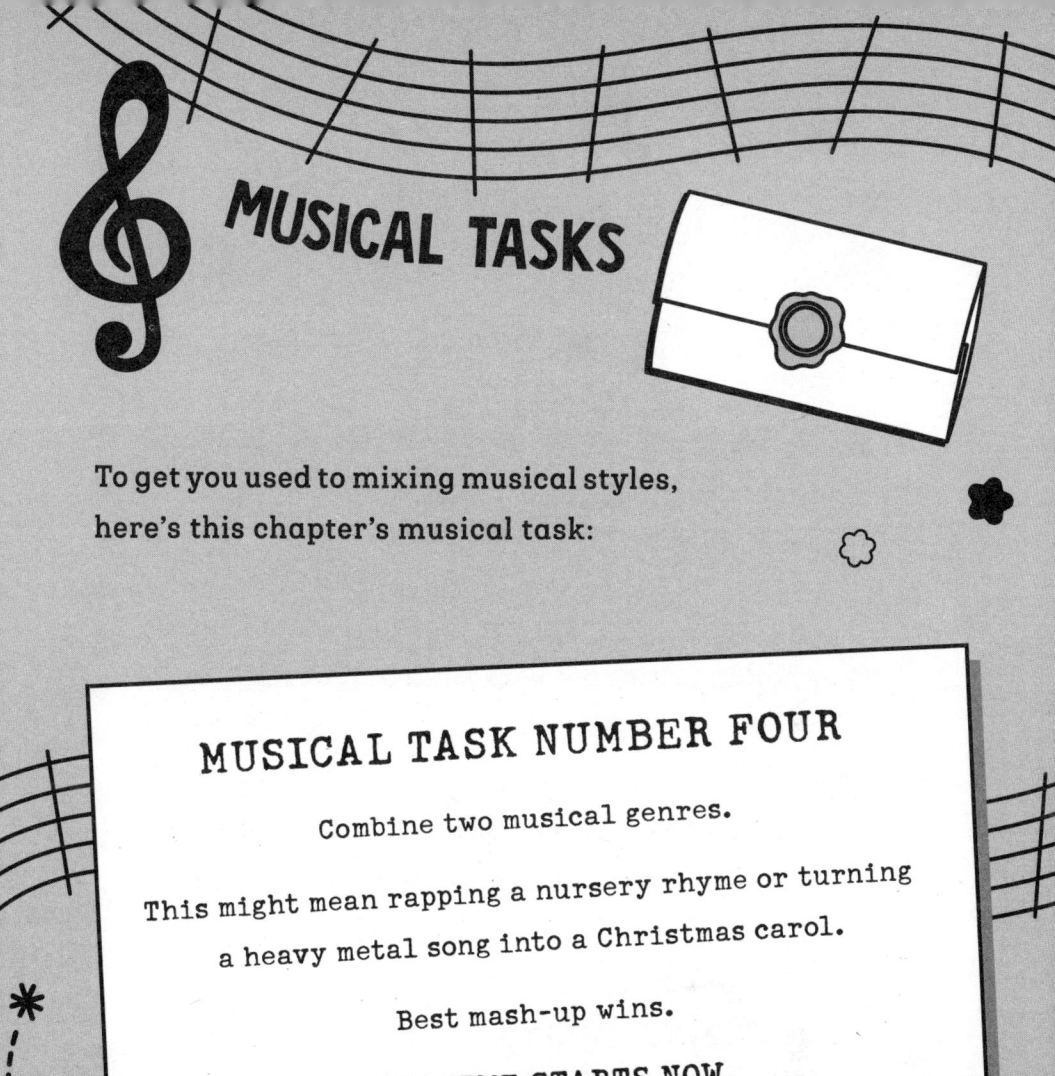

To get you used to mixing musical styles, here's this chapter's musical task:

MUSICAL TASK NUMBER FOUR

Combine two musical genres.

This might mean rapping a nursery rhyme or turning a heavy metal song into a Christmas carol.

Best mash-up wins.

YOUR TIME STARTS NOW.

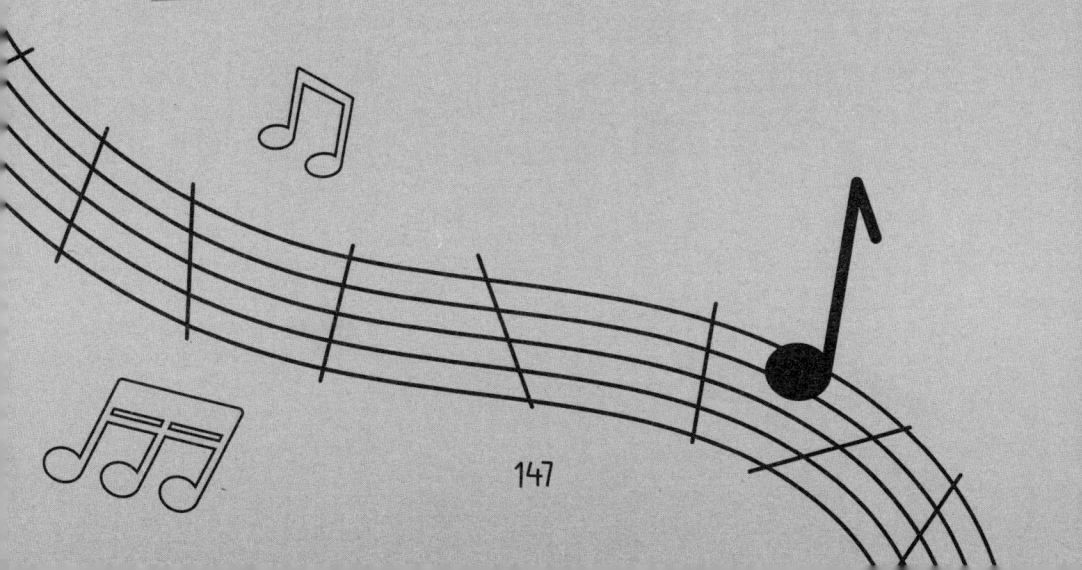

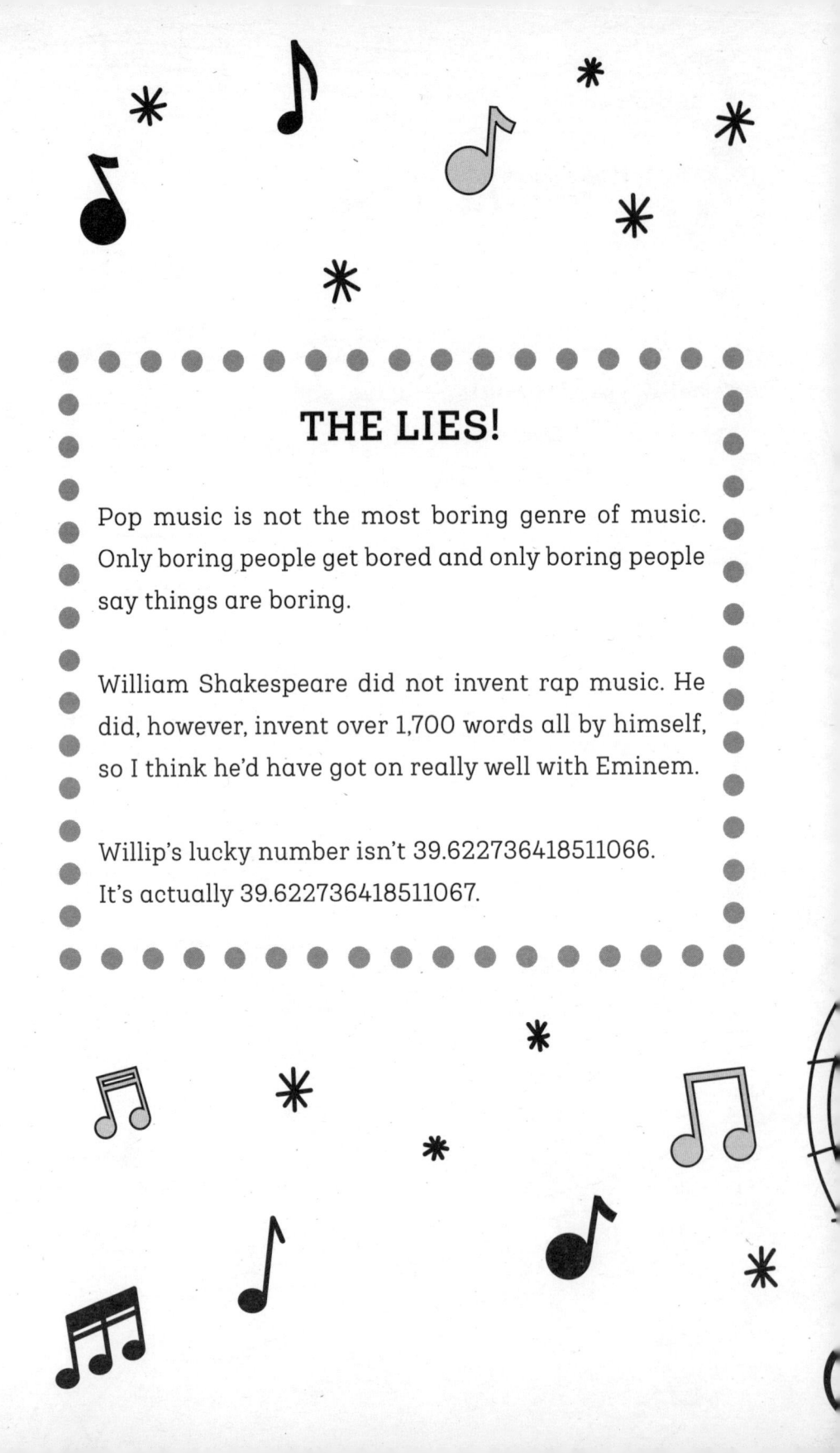

THE LIES!

Pop music is not the most boring genre of music. Only boring people get bored and only boring people say things are boring.

William Shakespeare did not invent rap music. He did, however, invent over 1,700 words all by himself, so I think he'd have got on really well with Eminem.

Willip's lucky number isn't 39.622736418511066. It's actually 39.622736418511067.

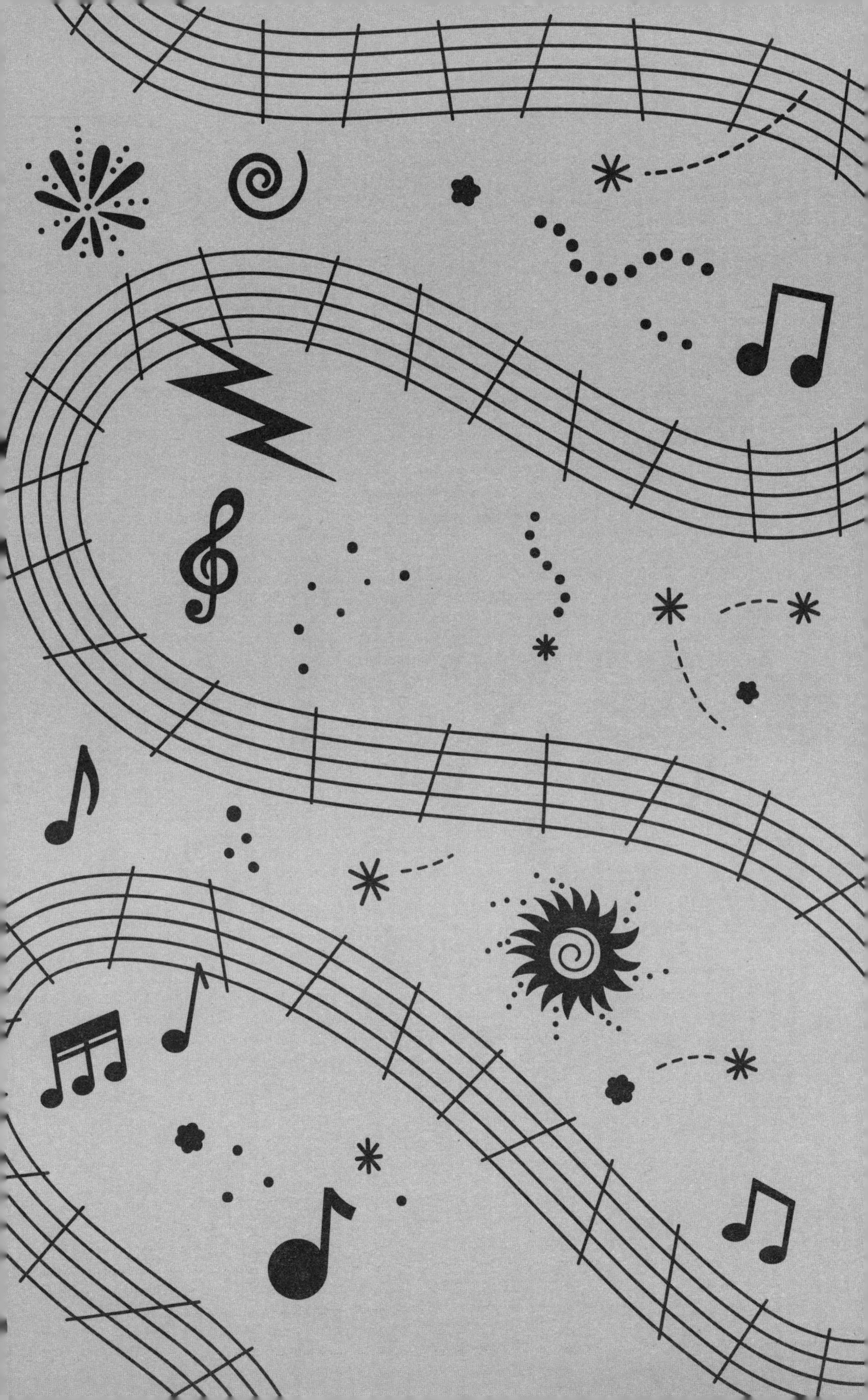

CHAPTER

FIVE

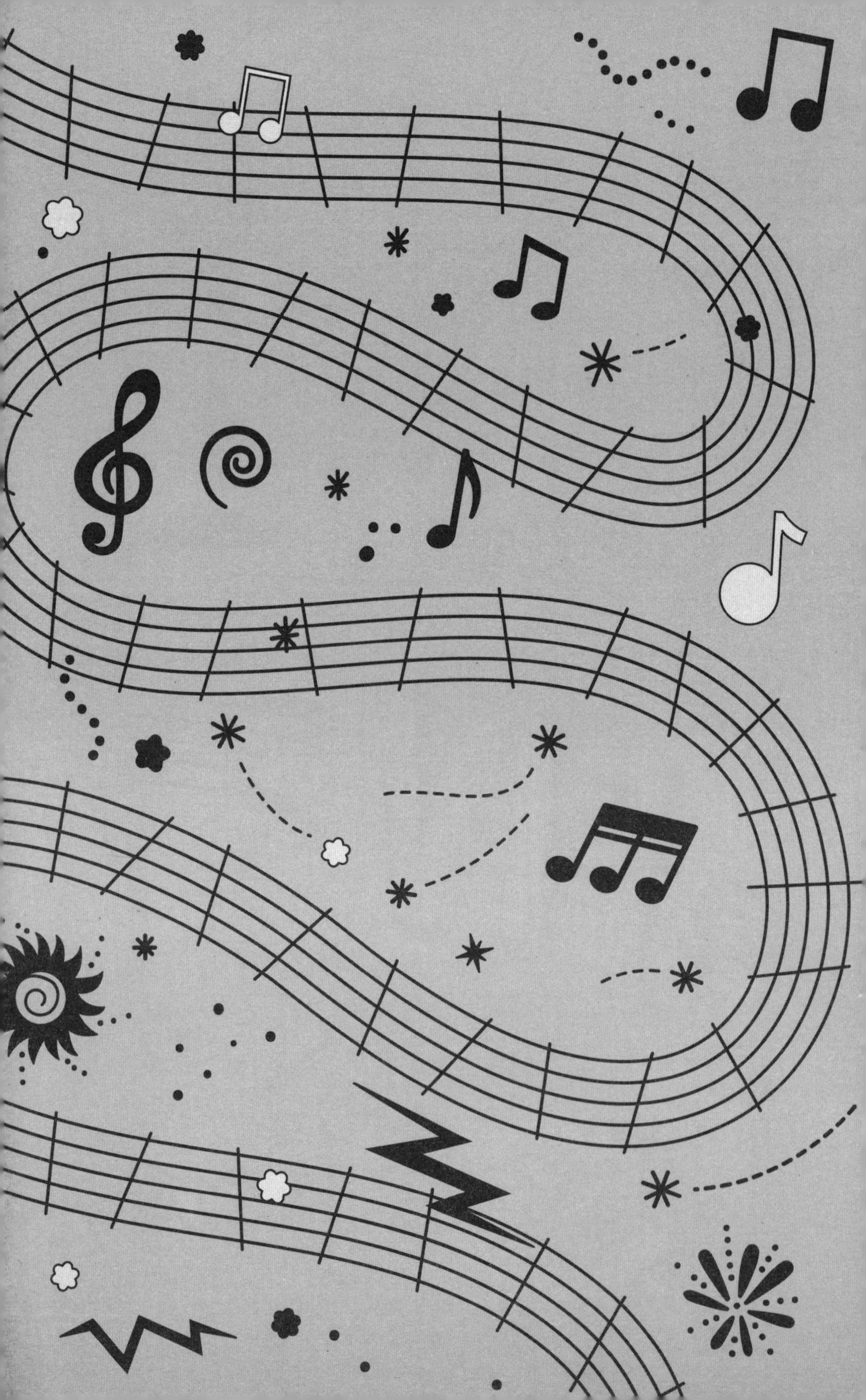

WHERE SHOULD I PLAY MY MUSIC?

Going to watch and listen to music being played is one of the best things to do with your free time. I say that partly because I'm in a band and we want people to come and watch us play our music, but mainly because it's true. Live music is as fun as live football, as thrilling as the cinema and even more sociable than the zoo.

A musical performance is called a concert, and if you haven't been to one before you should ask your parents to take you to one immediately. Straight after reading this chapter. Your first concert could be a pop concert, a rock show, an opera or a whole music festival. It could be put on by professional musicians in a football stadium or your mates in a park. The main thing is, you and a whole load of other people will get to hear music played live, and that's always exciting.

To make things even more thrilling, concerts have happened in some really odd places: the roofs of buildings, inside prisons, on Antarctica, even underwater! And I bet you've never heard of the cat who crashed a very posh classical music concert? You will soon.

Nobody knows when the very first live musical performance took place. Presumably the first cavemen clapped their hands and shouted for a bit, before realizing one of them could sing. Then they started belting out the theme tune to *The Flintstones*. And so live music was born!

Now we also use live music to celebrate – whether it's a birthday, a holiday or a wedding. Sometimes we also play music to acknowledge that we're sad. In England, sports fans always sing 'Sweet Caroline' when we're not going to win a football tournament, for example. Music is a powerful force that can bring people and communities together.

If you want to get out there and make some noise to crowds cheering your name, you're going to need to work out which venue is calling your name. And we're here to help!

BAND CHAT

Alex: How does music bring us all together?

Band: Music helps us fall in love and strengthens our communities. Think about singing in school assemblies or churches, round a Christmas tree or at a party. It's often the thing that unites us.

Soldiers around the world sing and play music together during wartime because it provides comfort. Centuries ago Roman soldiers used to chant tunes while marching to keep their spirits up and the songs sung by soldiers in the First World War (like It's a Long Way to Tipperary) are still known today.

Band: Although it's worth noting that in Monaco the national orchestra is actually bigger than their army. (They have eighty-five musicians and eighty-two soldiers.) Still, as Alex proves all the time, you don't have to be good at music to sing a song.

Alex: I am good at music, thank you. I just do it without actually learning any instruments, unlike you lot. And, by the way, that really is a tiny army. How do you know all this stuff?

Band: Oh, we read another book all about music.

Alex: Shhhh . . . this is the ONLY book about music, remember?

Band: Good point. Hey, look out of the window! There's a weasel riding on the back of a woodpecker!

Alex: I looked and there it was. Remarkable. But back to the book. What makes live music so special?

Band: Listening to music at home by yourself is great, but it's completely different to it being played in front of you. There is something more exciting about live music. Often it's louder (which is always better) and the atmosphere is electric, because the audience sing along and cheer. There is also the added excitement of something maybe going wrong...

Take American rock band the Foo Fighters, one of the biggest live rock bands in the world. Their lead singer, Dave Grohl, was on stage in Gothenburg in Sweden and wanted to get as close to the edge of the stage as possible, to connect to the fans. Unfortunately he tripped just at the wrong moment and fell about seven metres from the stage. He got up and tried to continue but found it wasn't that easy with a broken leg. For the rest of the tour Dave had to sit on a hastily constructed 'rock' throne, with his limb in a cast.

Alex: Can I just say that I am a much more responsible lead singer than Dave Grohl. I always stay right in the middle of the stage, I never try to sing difficult high notes and I usually wear shin pads just in case.

Band: Amazingly all those things are true. But audiences don't just enjoy live music because of the mistakes. Musicians playing live can be a magical thing; some can improvise or add extra bits to their performance that their band mates can then pick up and run with, adding in and changing things themselves. It's a little bit like watching a brilliant team goal in football. You don't know what's going to happen next, but the players manage to work together to make something unique and special.

In music this means a live performance can turn a song into something completely different to the original recorded version. It won't always be better, but it's often more fun. When we perform live we like to improvise and mess about musically. It keeps us interested, keeps the audience on their toes and often confuses Alex, as he never really knows what's going on.

Alex: Pardon? I don't understand.

Band: To get to a point where a band is comfortable improvising live on stage takes many, many hours of practice. You might have heard people say that you need to do 10,000 hours of practice to become a world-beater at anything, be that saxophone or sewing or colouring in.

Band: We've calculated that the Horne Section musicians have done exactly 10,000 hours of practice between us, and we're pretty sure that still counts. Even if Alex only did one of those hours and the rest of us shared out the other 9,999.

ALEX HAS LEFT THE CONVERSATION.

LIVE MUSIC FACT:

BEYONCÉ IS A GREAT EXAMPLE OF A VERY TALENTED PERSON WHO HAD LOTS AND LOTS OF PRACTICE AND TOUGH TRAINING BEFORE SHE WAS FAMOUS. SHE ONCE SAID:

> My father, who was also my manager, made me run a mile while singing so I would be able to perform on stage without becoming exhausted.

WE THINK THIS IS GREAT PARENTING AND IF WE WERE STILL CHILDREN WITH HEALTHY KNEES WE'D DEFINITELY BE SINGING WHILE SPRINTING TOO.

THE WEIRDEST PLACES WE'VE PLAYED MUSIC

An international stadium tour is when a band or musician travels all over the world performing in stadiums. For global stars such as Ed Sheeran, Irish rock band U2 or South Korean boy band BTS, their tours can go on for months or sometimes even years, and involve playing at stadiums across most continents to enormous crowds.

BIG GIG FACT:

BRITISH ROCK STAR ROD STEWART HOLDS THE CURRENT WORLD RECORD FOR THE BIGGEST GIG OF ALL TIME. HE ONCE PLAYED ON NEW YEAR'S EVE TO 3.5 MILLION PEOPLE ON COPACABANA BEACH IN BRAZIL. THAT'S THE SAME AS THE ENTIRE POPULATION OF URUGUAY TURNING UP TO SEE ONE SHOW!

When you're starting out as a musician (before you become a world-famous star), you might find you want to do every gig that comes your way, even when it's not quite as glamorous as an international tour. As young jazz musicians, fresh out of music college, the members of the Horne Section began playing in very small places, sometimes to just one man and his dog in a pub (or to some unimpressed diners in a Pizza Express).

We've also done our fair share of unusual shows. One of Mark's first jobs was to play a series of Christmas gigs in an old castle, dressed up in a monk's costume complete with cloak and fake bald patch. He was asked to play medieval music but all he could think of was the Henry VIII classic 'Greensleeves'. So he played that over and over again, much to the annoyance of the confused diners who really just wanted to hear Christmas songs.

> 'Greensleeves' was written more than 400 years ago. Henry VIII claimed to have written the music, but he was famously both boastful and very keen on beheading people. Our guess is that he made one of his musical jesters write it and threatened to chop off the poor man's head if he dared to take any credit. Just like Alex does today.

Oi!

Little Joe Auckland, our trumpeter, once had a gig playing his trumpet in one of the grandest and most iconic buildings in London, St Paul's Cathedral, which was built more than 300 years ago. This historic cathedral is famous for its dome. You can actually walk round the inside of this dome and, thirty metres up from the cathedral floor, there's an area called the Whispering Gallery. It's called this because it carries sound around the walls so well that you can whisper to a friend standing on the other side and still be heard. Unfortunately Joe didn't play his trumpet quietly. He's not really good enough to play his trumpet quietly yet. So the whole of London heard him tootle away.

Joe was also once excited to be in a show where everyone had to play dressed as a superhero. When he arrived, he was handed his costume for Robin, i.e. Batman's sidekick, i.e. the most pathetic of all the superheroes.

For one whole year our drummer Ben had to dress as a Second World War soldier in a jazz band. It's not what he thought he'd do as a musician but it did turn out to be fun.

We've gradually worked our way up to playing in stadiums and festivals all over the world. Now we are lucky enough to perform huge shows at places like Wembley Stadium, where the England football team also play, and the Pyramid Stage at Glastonbury, which is the most famous stage at the most famous festival in the world. So just keep working hard and see where your musical journey takes you!

THE WEIRDEST MUSICAL LOCATIONS IN THE WORLD, EVER!

As we've already discovered, music isn't always performed on boring stages in boring venues. Over the years, musicians have played in some weird and wonderful places, from outer space to under the sea.

Paul McCartney grew up in Liverpool, playing football and guitar with his friends. By the time he was twenty-seven years old he was already one of the most famous and influential musical artists ever, as one of the lead singers of The Beatles. Probably the greatest-ever band, The Beatles once had all top five songs in the American charts, as well as the UK number one **SINGLE** and album. They've sold over a billion records.

Amazingly they were only actually together for *seven* years. They performed their last-ever concert on the roof of their studio offices in the middle of London. This happened in 1968 and was their first public performance for two years, which meant it was a complete surprise for fans. Two of the band also wore their wives' coats because it was so windy on the roof, so this was even more confusing for a lot of busy people trying to get home from work!

The Beatles were the first artists to have a live gig broadcast in space when their song 'Good Day Sunshine' was used to wake up the crew of the International Space Station (a station orbiting Earth with astronauts living and working inside). Presumably they were warned beforehand, otherwise that would have almost certainly annoyed some of the astronauts, and that's never a good idea.

Speaking of astronauts, the Canadian astronaut Chris Hadfield took his guitar up to the International Space Station and recorded a video of himself singing a song called 'Space Oddity' by English singer-songwriter David Bowie. This was the first music video to be recorded in space!

Next up is probably the highest gig ever performed (although there have been other attempts). Big-hatted British funk band Jamiroquai played a gig in a specially designed Boeing 757 aeroplane at 33,000 feet in the air. The band played five songs during the flight from Munich to Athens and the 200 passengers were invited to a special after-party when they landed.

Unfortunately their attempt was beaten three years later by posh British singer James Blunt, who did the same thing but 9,000 feet higher. And he then had *his* record smashed by 80s stars Kim Wilde and Tony Hadley who did a gig on a jumbo jet at 43,000 feet for Comic Relief!

> An actual gig in actual outer space seems like the next step. And we are definitely up for it if NASA is reading this. That is a big if unfortunately.

At the other end of the spectrum, holding the record for lowest gig ever, is Georgian and British singer-songwriter Katie Melua, who did a gig 303 metres below sea level on a Norwegian oil rig. (An oil rig is a huge structure out at sea that is used by tough engineers to drill into the seabed for oil.) Katie sings a song about bicycles in Beijing, but hopefully on this occasion she sang the Disney classic 'Under the Sea'.

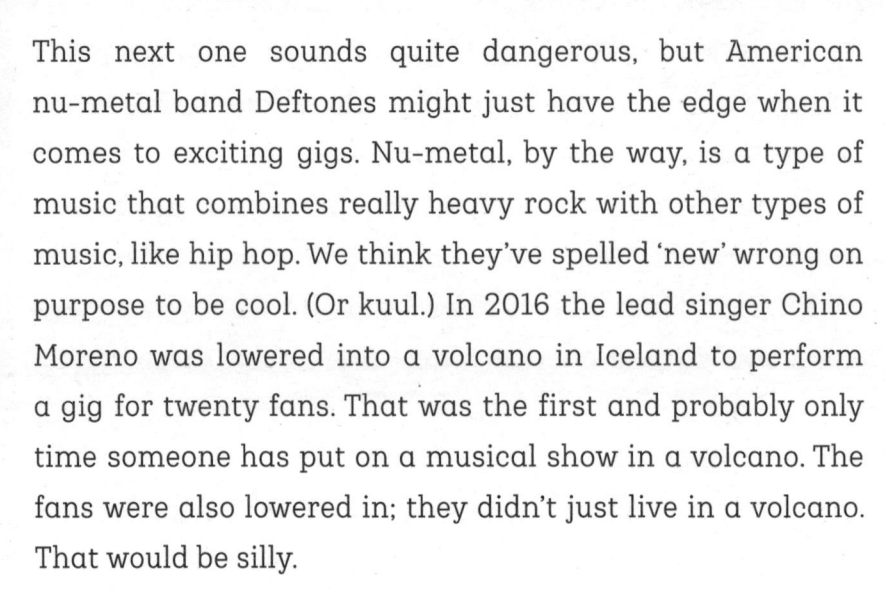

This next one sounds quite dangerous, but American nu-metal band Deftones might just have the edge when it comes to exciting gigs. Nu-metal, by the way, is a type of music that combines really heavy rock with other types of music, like hip hop. We think they've spelled 'new' wrong on purpose to be cool. (Or kuul.) In 2016 the lead singer Chino Moreno was lowered into a volcano in Iceland to perform a gig for twenty fans. That was the first and probably only time someone has put on a musical show in a volcano. The fans were also lowered in; they didn't just live in a volcano. That would be silly.

We're not suggesting you should always play songs somewhere really dangerous, but if you're just starting up, learning an instrument in your bedroom, hitting the drums in your parents' garage or playing the recorder in a school assembly, we hope these stories inspire you and remind you that when it comes to live music – nowhere is off limits!

BIG GIG FACT:

METALLICA IS AN AMERICAN BAND THAT FORMED IN 1981. THEY ARE ONE OF THE HEAVIEST OF ALL THE HEAVY METAL BANDS, AND THEY DECIDED IN 2013 TO DO A SERIES OF GIGS ON ALL SEVEN CONTINENTS IN ONE YEAR, ENDING THE RECORD-BREAKING FEAT WITH A CONCERT IN ANTARCTICA. APPARENTLY 300 CURIOUS PENGUINS TURNED UP BUT NOT MANY HUMANS.

DANGER

THE MOST DANGEROUS MUSIC IN HISTORY

We've mentioned some fairly risky live music events but most of these took place without any real physical harm coming to anyone, apart from Dave Grohl (and we think he probably enjoyed it). But if we look back a little further, we can find some even more dangerous music-related stories!

In April 1912 a huge ship called the *Titanic* set sail from Southampton in England to New York in the USA. Five days later it crashed into an iceberg and sank. Only 715 of the 2,200 passengers survived. Members of the London Symphony Orchestra were booked to perform on the doomed liner, but were fortunate enough to change boats at the last minute.

Others weren't so lucky. Eight unfortunate musicians were on the ship, where they were paid to play for the diners. As the ship sank, they carried on playing for as long as they possibly could, in an effort to calm the terrified passengers. The whole group were later recognized for their heroism.

Twenty-five years later, in 1937, a man called Louis Vierne was giving an organ recital in the Notre-Dame cathedral in Paris. Unfortunately the renowned musician had a heart attack immediately after playing the last chord of the piece and collapsed on the instrument's pedals. The organ itself seemed to understand the tragic situation – it made a final noisy groan as Louis died.

Musical instruments can be terrifying. In 2006 a man in Florida was killed by a trumpet that fell on him from a fourth-floor balcony. Pianos also have a terrible habit of squashing people (mostly on telly and particularly in *Tom and Jerry* cartoons) and every year over a thousand people in Wales alone get their heads stuck in the strings of harps and end up starving to death.

Finally if we head back thousands of years, we find our Celtic ancestors (warrior tribes who came to the UK from across western Europe) playing a brass instrument called a carnyx, particularly during battles. The instrument was very tall and shaped like an animal's head. To play it, you blew in one end and the sound came out of the other end, which would have been about a metre above the player. Apparently the noise was so dreadful that if a few of them were played together it would scare off the enemy before a fight had even begun.

> Alex isn't allowed to play instruments in our shows for a similar reason.

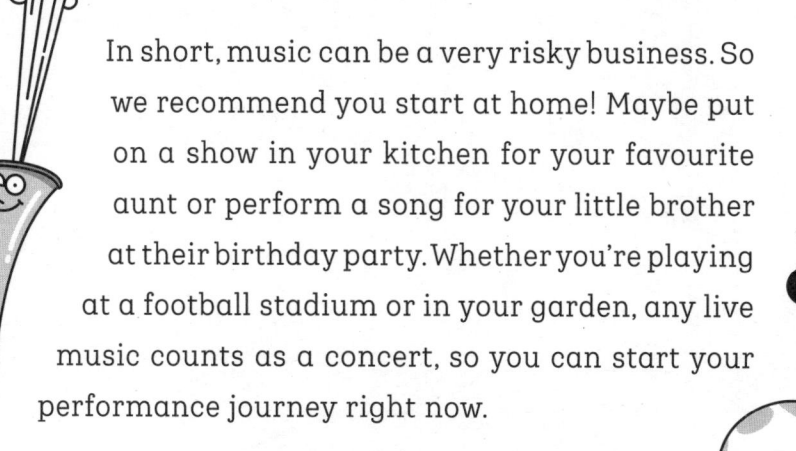

In short, music can be a very risky business. So we recommend you start at home! Maybe put on a show in your kitchen for your favourite aunt or perform a song for your little brother at their birthday party. Whether you're playing at a football stadium or in your garden, any live music counts as a concert, so you can start your performance journey right now.

> But what about the cat?

Ah yes, *the cat!* Well, there certainly can be dangers with live music, but it can also be the most calming thing in the world. In 2020 a stray cat was enjoying an orchestra's concert in Istanbul so much it wandered right into the heart of the orchestra, pottered about among the musicians and sniffed various cellists. Clearly completely relaxed, it eventually settled in the best seat in the house, on the conductor's podium, right at the front of the stage.

So be like that cat. Explore the world through music, make friends and have fun.

Speaking of which, here is your next task. Rope in your friends and family for this one and see how you get on.

MUSICAL TASKS

MUSICAL TASK NUMBER FIVE

Perform some music in the most unusual location.

Weirdest gig wins.

YOUR TIME STARTS NOW.

THE LIES!

At the start of this chapter we said we read about the Monaco army in another book. That's not true. We've never read another book. Why would we when we've written the only book on music that anyone could ever need? We actually found that fact on the internet. When we looked a little harder we found that the Monaco army actually has 250 active soldiers in it, so saying that their national orchestra is bigger than their army was also a lie... But that's not nearly as interesting.

While on the subject of the internet, I have to confess that we haven't yet played at Wembley Stadium or Glastonbury's Pyramid Stage, and I didn't actually see a weasel riding a woodpecker out of my window. But this did actually happen in 2015 and was captured by amateur photographer Martin Le-May. Ask a parent to find the animal images for you online and you won't be disappointed.

Finally it is true that various musical instruments have caused injuries and even deaths throughout history. All the examples in this chapter did actually happen. All except the harp one. Although we still recommend that you be careful and keep your head out of any harps.

CHAPTER

SIX

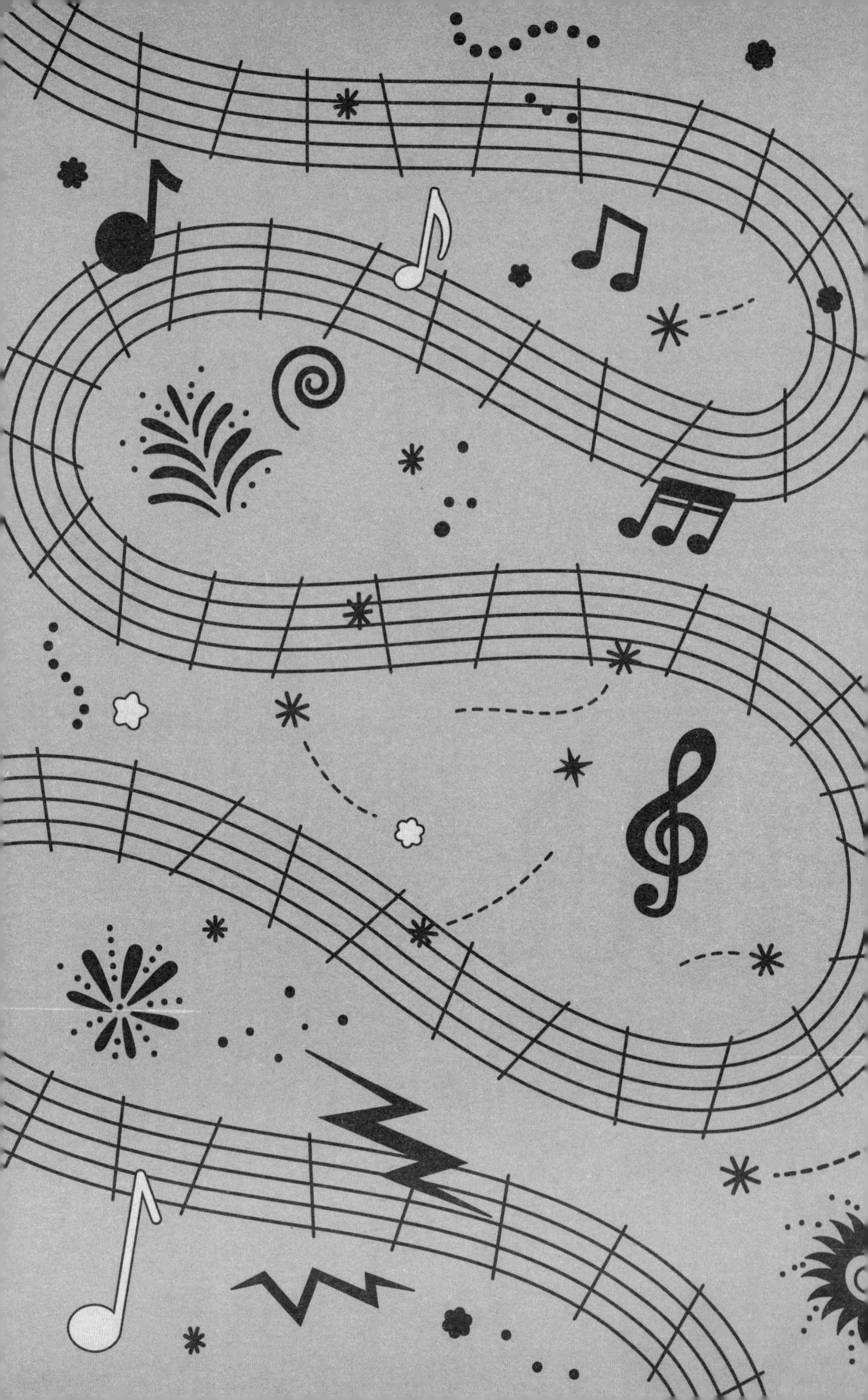

HOW WILL PEOPLE HEAR MY MUSIC?

So far you've learned how to make music, how to play different genres of music and where you might be able to play your music. But we've not yet talked about how music is passed on. You can't see, touch, taste or smell music (although there is a certain sort of sound we all make that you definitely can smell – more of that later), so how does music spread across the world so fast?

Personally I have no idea. I have too many other things to worry about like what I'm having for lunch and where my socks are, so here are the band to tell you all about how music moves around the world.

> I'd like sausages and mashed potato and my best sporty socks please.

WHERE DID THE FIRST MUSIC COME FROM?

Some people think that early humans were making music before they learned to speak. Charles Darwin, a clever scientist from the 1800s, said:

> Musical tones and rhythm were used by our half-human ancestors, during the season of courtship, when animals of all kinds are excited not only by love, but by strong passions of jealousy, rivalry and triumph.

DARWIN

So hundreds of thousands of years ago our great-great-great-great-great-etc.-grandparents would have sung melodies without words (a bit like birds do) as a way of communicating. They would warble tunes when they felt strong emotions, rather than saying 'I feel very angry about this'. That's what Darwin thought anyway.

A philosopher called Herbert Spencer, who was also coming up with theories in the 1800s, had this to say:

Music arose from the cadences of emotional speech.

SPENCER

What he means is that when people speak, it is slightly musical to begin with, in the way the rhythm and pitch can change. He argued that music actually grew from words, not the other way round. A good way to test his theory would be to ask someone to say 'hello, how are you?'. Now try to mimic the rhythm, pitch and tone of what they said with 'La, la. La, la, la'. There. You're singing! So we can be melodic without even realizing!

It's a bit like the chicken and the egg problem; we don't know whether music or speech came first. But either way, people have been making music for longer than we can remember, so let's see how these tunes have been passed on through the generations.

THE OLDEST SONGS

The very first songs were sung before people could write. They were sung thousands of years ago, before computers, synthesizers, hole punches and even books. Many folk songs, for example, were never written down, which sadly means that a whole load of songs have been lost forever.

> This isn't always a bad thing, though, especially when songs are rubbish – it's sort of a shame that there's no way to lose 'Baby Shark'.

But despite people not having pens and computers and hole punches, lots of songs that were made hundreds of years ago have still survived to today. And that's largely because of our funny old ears, who teamed up with our mouths to pass the songs on from generation to generation.

Parents taught songs to their children, who later taught the same songs to their nieces and nephews, who later taught them to their best friend's parrot trainer. Some of the most famous English folk songs and nursery rhymes that we still sing today were remembered and passed on in exactly this way – from mouth to ear – for hundreds of years.

We're guessing you've never written down the words and musical notes for 'The Grand Old Duke of York' but one day you might find yourself singing it to the next generation of kids. And that is exactly what has happened for years and years and years. People have sung this tune to each other for so long that we don't actually know who the Grand Old Duke of York was! It might be a soldier called Frederick, who was born in 1763; it might be King James II, born in 1633; or it might even have been a Duke of York called Richard who was born more than 600 years ago and lived from 1411 to 1460!

When pencils and biros and hole punches were eventually invented, people finally started to write song lyrics down. It's a bit like jokes. People were asking why the chicken crossed the road for years before it was finally written down in a New York magazine called *The Knickerbocker* in 1847. And since then, friends have kept saying it to other friends, dads to kids, kids to teachers, teachers to doctors, doctors to patients and so on. Then it was finally written in joke books and on the internet, which means our chicken hero will never be forgotten.

About 4,000 years ago musicians started writing instructions on how to sing songs too. In medieval times, about a thousand years ago, composers began to use musical notation so that everyone would be able to play the tunes exactly as intended – and that's the system we still use today. We covered this in Chapter 3, so for now we're going to stick with the people who were just singing to each other a long time ago because that's more like the sort of thing we get up to. The Horne Section are not renowned for their complicated compositions. We're more into mucking about, having fun and not spending too long writing things down.

*

> I am not in favour of all this 'fun', and I definitely do enjoy writing things down, especially when it comes to telling people about music in an actual book.

FARTY FACTS ABOUT OLD MUSIC

DO YOU KNOW WHAT 'FLATULISM' IS? IF NOT, DEFINITELY ASK YOUR PARENTS TO DEMONSTRATE.

Aha! Now you know. Some people find it disgusting, but we do have to discuss it at some point. This is a book about *all* music. And flatulism is essentially farting in a creative, amusing or musical way, so it's definitely earned its place in this book.

About 900 years ago, in the year 1150, a medieval flatulist called Roland the Farter was Henry II's court jester. Roland's job was to perform a piece of music called 'One Jump and One Whistle and One Fart' for the king every Christmas. (We're sure there's someone in your class who could do a similar job for your headteacher.) In return for farting, the king gave Roland the Farter a massive house with a massive garden. And this is what we mean when we say music can be for anyone – you don't even need an instrument.

> Lucky Roland.

> Smelly disgusting Roland, you mean.

> Well, I happen to think that the guy is a legend.

There was another man, born a long time after Roland in 1857, called Le Pétomane, who also tried his hand at musical farting. Le Pétomane was a French entertainer who performed at the Moulin Rouge, a famous nightclub in Paris, and he delighted audiences that included the serious psychologist Sigmund Freud and the actual king of Belgium, Leopold II. Le Pétomane's job title was professional farter and there were even a musical and a film made about his life. You might be wondering, if you can do farting performances for a living, what's the point of going to school? Maybe you should ask your teachers to teach you how to do musical farts instead of your usual classes...

BALL(AD) GAMES

A cross between ballet and salad, the word 'ballad' should mean a dancing lettuce, but it's actually a 'slow song' or a song that tells a story. In the fifteenth century ballads were used as a way of spreading information and news. A ballad would be written and printed on huge sheets of paper that were sold to travelling musicians. These musicians would then sing them in different places, spreading the news of the world. Ballads were a bit like Twitter or TikTok but larger, longer and louder.

Love stories, funny stories, stories about folk legends such as Robin Hood, historical tales, religious stories, news about politics, fashion, battles or just general gossip could all be covered in a medieval ballad.

But our favourite is definitely . . . **MURDER BALLADS!** For these dramatic news songs, songwriters or 'minstrels', would go to courts to witness murder trials. Like musical journalists, they would write up the details of the case as a song, then sell the sheet music and sing the songs at public hangings!

Murder ballads were so popular that the songs would often travel all the way around the world. Musicians would hop on a boat from England to America with songs they knew or songs they had written themselves. And once they arrived, they would have a whole new audience. Some murder ballads that were written hundreds of years ago in the UK are actually still sung in America today!

TECH TIME!

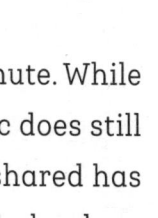

Let's fast-forward right up to now – this very minute. While we do sing songs to one another today, and music does still spread right across the world, the way music is shared has changed a lot since the days of murder ballads. Technology has moved so fast, especially in this century, that not only are large pieces of paper no longer needed, nothing physical is needed any more at all.

The most common way to listen to music today is to ask a smart speaker to play you a specific song by a particular singer. You could even ask it to play any song from a particular genre of music, and the device will do exactly that. It's basically magic.

There are many other devices available for listening to music nowadays. You can hear songs on your TV, a tablet, a phone or a computer. You may even use a CD player, but I'm sure the next generation will think you're incredibly old for doing so.

HOW DO COOL PEOPLE RECORD MUSIC TODAY?

If you want to perform an old-fashioned murder ballad, all you really need to do is find a story, write down some words on a big piece of paper, go to your friend's house and sing it to them. But the songs on your smart speaker and the songs you hear on the radio today have gone through a slightly more complicated process. Here's how it works:

The musicians head to a recording studio. These are some of the coolest places in the whole world. They come in all shapes and sizes but usually have at least three rooms.

1 **A CONTROL ROOM.** This is where the 'engineers' or the 'producers' sit. We met music producers back in Chapter 4. These are the adults who work in recording studios, but they don't seem like adults because they don't wear suits or have showers. They are like modern-day magicians and they sit in the control room recording the music played in the live room, making the songs sound the best they possibly can. There are between one and three computers in the room and lots of devices with many, many smart switches and slidey buttons that control the volume of all the instruments and microphones.

2

A LIVE ROOM where musicians play their songs. There are instruments in the room, plus a load of microphones.

3

A ROOM WHERE PEOPLE DRINK TEA and play table tennis and sit on a leather sofa. Chill-out time!

BAND CHAT

Alex: Why do you need all those machines and magicians? A song is a song, isn't it? It's either a good song or a stupid song, like the ones we write?

Band: No. Even good songs can sound awful if not recorded properly. And you can *really* improve songs (even ours!) with the right recording techniques. Recording studios are brilliant places. With the help of a recording engineer, when you record a song in a studio you can change how each instrument sounds or even edit out part of a song you don't like. You could edit out coughs, burps and bum notes.

> Contrary to its name, a bum note is not a fart but a note that a musician plays by accident.

Band: Recording engineers can make you sound like you are singing in a tiny toilet cubicle or a big boomy concert hall. An engineer might even decide to have some instruments coming out of the left speaker and some coming out of the right speaker when the listener hears the final recording. They can shape and edit the recording so that you can hear every instrument clearly. People working in studios often talk about making sure everything 'hangs together' or 'sits'. Engineers can help musicians make sad songs sound warm and fuzzy or help make scary music sound even more terrifying.

Almost anything is possible in a studio. There's even a device you can use if your singer is a little off-key and out of tune. This is called auto-tune.

Alex: I don't think anyone's ever had to use auto-tune on my voice.

Band: Oh, we agree. You have a beautiful voice, Alex Horne. Definitely you do.

ALEX HAS LEFT THE CONVERSATION.

THE PEOPLE YOU GET IN A RECORDING STUDIO

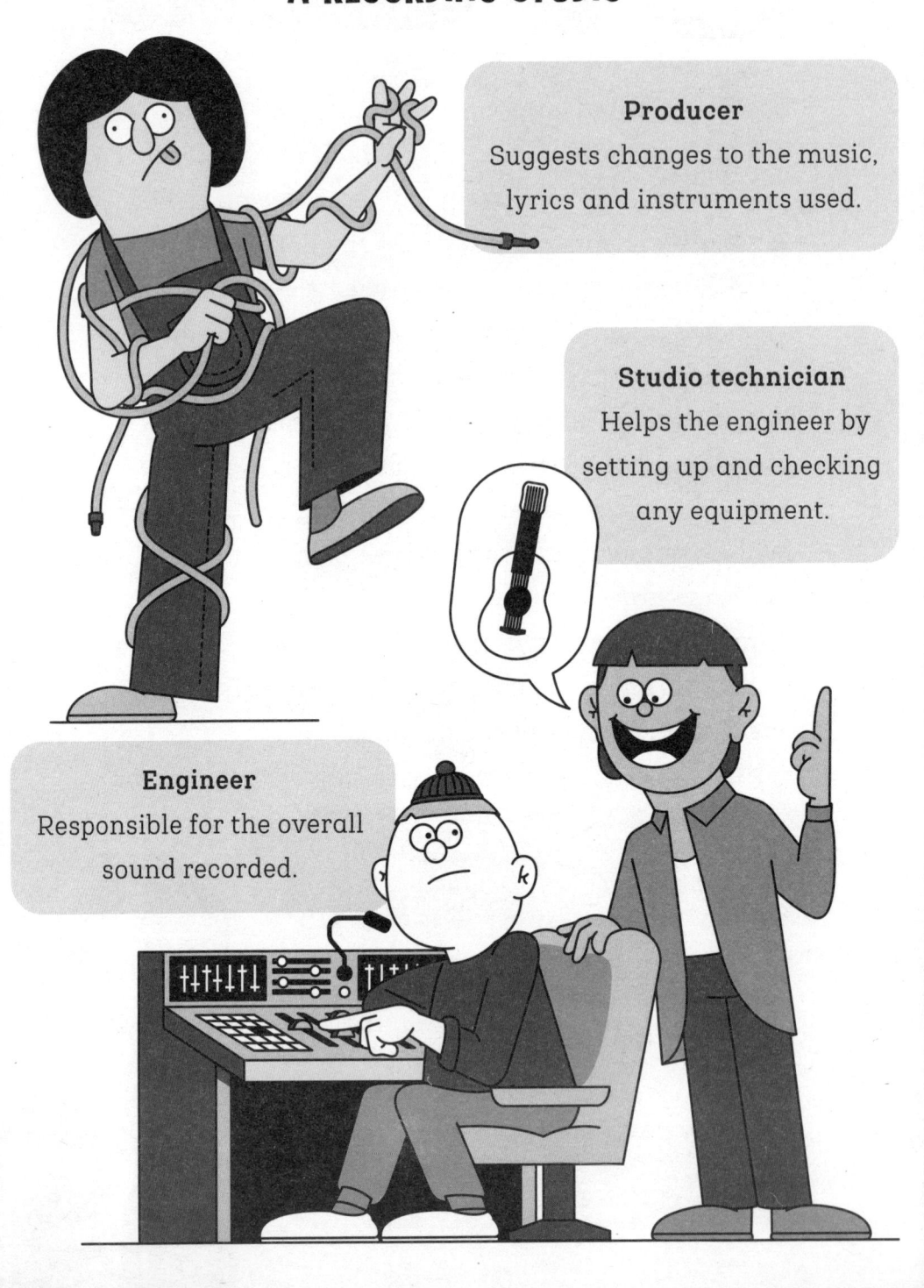

Producer
Suggests changes to the music, lyrics and instruments used.

Studio technician
Helps the engineer by setting up and checking any equipment.

Engineer
Responsible for the overall sound recorded.

THE GEAR YOU GET IN A RECORDING STUDIO

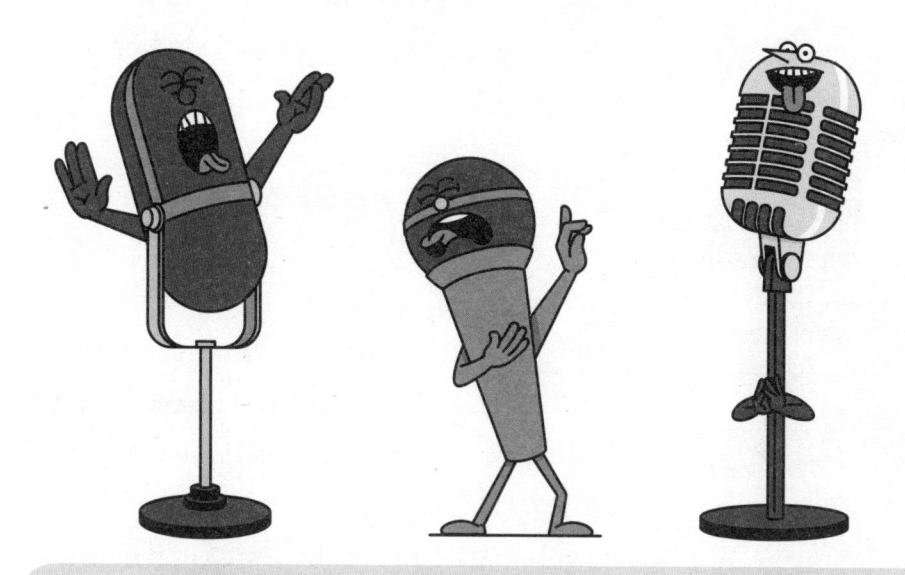

Microphones

There are hundreds of different microphones. Certain microphones are good at recording certain instruments. A recording engineer will know which microphone to use for each job. Microphones can cost anywhere from 1p to one quadrillion pounds. So start saving your pocket money now if you'd like a big one. When you speak, shout or sing into the microphone, the microphone converts the sound wave into an electrical signal that can be recorded via the mixing desk.

> ALL this 'converting the sound wave into an electrical signal' sounds really boring. Shall we go and play table tennis?

Cables
Cables send the electrical signals. They are plugged into each microphone and these are then plugged into the mixing desk.

Please can I use this as a Lasso? Pretty please?

Mixing Desk
Seeing a mixing desk for the first time is like boarding a very cool spaceship. A musical spaceship piloted by a recording engineer. This desk is a huge electronic table as big as a car. It has thousands of brightly coloured buttons, wires, twiddly knobs, flashing lights and switches. Every one of these has its own little job in changing the recorded sound in some way.

Computers. Great, that's a relief. Let's play fortnite.

Computer
Please ignore him. Studios didn't use to have computers, but now every studio has to have a computer to record the music into. This is where your song can be saved and kept until the next time you'd like to hear it.

Speakers

In studios these are sometimes called 'monitors'. Everyone can sit around and hear what they've recorded through these.

Headphones

Speakers for your ears. Stick 'em on your head and listen to what you've done without anyone else knowing what you're up to.

Microphone stands

To balance the expensive microphones on.

Other bits and bobs

When we record in studios we try to pretend that we know what the recording engineer is doing as they twiddle all those knobs – because recording engineers, like spaceship pilots, are cool.

LEARN YOUR LINGO!

If you are going to go to a recording studio it will help you feel at home if you practise some complicated phrases. These will ensure that people think you know *exactly* what you are doing. Try these for size:

> I THINK THE BASS DRUM NEEDS A BIT OF COMPRESSION.

> IT SOUNDS A BIT BOXY AT THE MOMENT, MAYBE ADD SOME REVERB – HAVE YOU GOT ANY DECENT PLATE REVERBS?

> IT WOULD BE GOOD TO TIGHTEN THE WHOLE THING UP.

> MAYBE YOU COULD BEEF UP THE VOCALS.

None of these mean anything but the producer will *definitely* nod and agree and then do something that makes the song sound no different at all.

The absolute best things in the recording studio are the chairs. You don't get rubbish normal chairs with four legs; instead you get chairs with . . . WHEELS! And they also SPIN AROUND!

Having said all that, if you want to record your own music right now, you don't need any of these things. You just need to read our song-writing tips in Chapter 7 then borrow a phone from someone, go to a voice-recorder app, press record and play your music.

Then listen to it back.

It'll sound just as good. But you won't get a fancy chair.

> You can use them to have races along the perfect shiny wooden floors. But then you have to pretend that the scratches on the floor were caused by the previous band.

A BRIEF HISTORY OF RECORDED MUSIC

We told you about murder ballads and professional farters, and then skipped straight ahead to wheelie chairs in recording studios. But there was a big chunk of time (about 800 years to be nearly precise) between these events, when the way we recorded and shared music changed a lot. So now we're going to take you through a timeline of how music sharing has evolved over the years...

RECORD PLAYERS

1877

American inventor Thomas Edison is most famous for coming up with the light bulb, which helped us to see better. But he also invented the phonograph in 1877 and that meant we could hear music better too.

The phonograph was the first device to reproduce recorded sound and it didn't even use electricity. It was a spinning cylinder that was rotated by turning a lever. There was tin foil wrapped round the cylinder. You would sing (or if you were Alex Horne, you would tunelessly

3 The invention of car stereos (machines in cars that could play sound, including cassette tapes) meant that people were able to choose the music they listened to in their cars.

4 You could rewind sound for the first time, simply by putting a pencil in the holes in the cassette tape and moving the tape back.

5 They just looked cool.

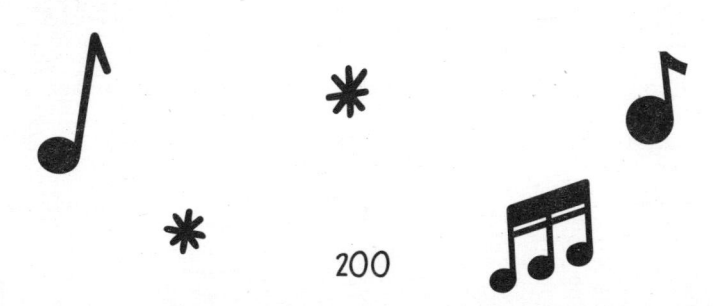

ON YOUR MARKS, CASSETTE, GO!

1963

In this year the cassette tape was born. These little bad boys revolutionized the world of music listening for five main reasons:

1 It was the first cheap music machine that you could record your own music on to. People made mix tapes by recording music from the radio or from record players, and putting tracks together to create their own combination of songs. Making someone a mix tape used to be a super-cool version of a love letter.

2 It was small. All small things are epic. For example Little Mix, Little Simz and Little Alex Horne, who is actually six foot five. The cassette was much smaller than records and you could listen to them with headphones and a portable personal stereo, such as a Sony Walkman. For the first time ever you could listen to music on the move and walk around town with your very own soundtrack!

RADIO GAGA

If people didn't have a record player, they might have had a radio. By the 1920s most American homes had radios, which brought news, music and laughter to human ears. The BBC started broadcasting in 1922 and during that decade families right across the UK also began listening to their own radios.

Old radio stations used electric signals that would send the sound recorded in the stations through the air as waves to huge poles called radio transmitters. These would then send those sounds out into the air as radio waves, and our own little radio machines would catch those radio waves with long metal poles called antennae, and we would be able to hear the news and songs being played in the stations.

Nowadays most of the radios you'll hear are DAB radios, which are equally mysterious (and confusing). The main difference is that the information is sent out as digital data, which means the sounds are somehow represented as loads and loads of ones and zeros, rather than waves. Your DAB radio can then understand the patterns of ones and zeros as sounds. When you write it down like that, it really doesn't make any sense, so let's move on and pretend we all understand how that works.

shout like a tone-deaf donkey), down one side of the cylinder. There was a needle inside the cylinder, and the vibrating sound waves of your voice would make the needle vibrate and etch lines into the foil. A needle on the other side could use the grooves in the tin foil to play back what you had just recorded!

1895

The first record player was produced in this year and became incredibly popular incredibly quickly. By the early 1900s many households were blasting out beautiful music using these machines! Based on Edison's phonograph technology, record players also used grooves to create sound. A record's grooves have undulations, hills, twists and turns, and these form the physical mark of the recorded sound. As the record spins, a needle (called a stylus) senses these grooves, picks up the vibrations and sends them to a device inside called a cartridge, which converts the movement into electrical energy. Finally the amplifier turns this energy into noise loud enough for us all to hear and dance to.

> Don't worry if this is all a bit complicated. Mainly it's all magic. Recorded music is just magic. There, we've said it. Take us to the jailhouse and lock us up.

MUSIC VIDEOS!
1981

A special music TV channel called MTV, or Music Television, was launched in America. It mainly played music videos and was presented by young cool people called 'video jockeys'. Because MTV became very popular, musicians started to spend more and more time and money making videos to accompany their songs. It was a great place for people to experience other people's music.

CDs
1982

CDs were first introduced in Japan, then a few months later in Europe. CDs are like vinyl records but a CD player uses lasers rather than a metal stylus to read the music. The CD player shoots lasers up to a spinning CD and the lasers use the information on the CD to convert it into sound.

And how exactly does this information get converted into sound? Well, you'll have to wait for the second book to find that out.

They definitely don't know.

MP3s
1987

Rather than songs being stored on a disc or a tape, they could now exist as a computer file, or an MP3, and these were first created in Germany. Unlike big records or chunky cassettes, these are tiny digital files that can be sent anywhere in the world. This meant people no longer had to wait for a record or CD or tape to hear a song.

NAPSTER
1999

A company called Napster allowed people to download an artist's music for free on the internet without the approval of the artists. Naughty Napster! Sales of music plummeted when people could access these illegal 'pirate' recordings and get music for free. Some people didn't notice at the time. Maybe they just thought Napster was a different name for a pirate hamster.

After long expensive legal battles Napster was shut down, but now we have legal streaming services like Spotify. These streaming companies have made agreements with record labels and musicians, which means they are allowed to give listeners access to their music.

BOULEVARD OF BROKEN STREAMS
2000

Broadband internet was rolled out in the UK. Before broadband the internet was slow. If you wanted to watch a video online or share it with a friend, you'd have to wait ages for it to load. But broadband meant that you could now send and share music, usually as MP3s, all over the world almost instantly!

2006

Spotify was founded. Using this new, faster internet, streaming services like Spotify, Apple Music and iTunes let us listen to billions of songs at the touch of a button.

NOW

These days people use all the above to share and listen to music, but some people still use huge pieces of paper. It depends on your personal preference. But when it comes to the Horne Section, Willip and Mark mainly use their phones to listen to music; Joe and Ben really like vinyl because they are stuck in the 1950s; Alex doesn't listen to music but he does like to wind the cassette tapes up with a pencil; and Ed uses CDs as ninja stars.

MUSICAL TASKS

MUSICAL TASK NUMBER SIX

Record a piece of music using things from your kitchen.

If you don't have a recording device yourself, ask your friends or family. One of them will probably have a voice-recorder app on their phone.

Capture the best tune you can make using pots and pans, whisks and spoons, rice and cereal or whatever you can lay your hands on.

Most delicious music wins.

YOUR TIME STARTS NOW.

THE LIES!

Luckily microphones don't cost a quadrillion pounds. Unluckily they also don't cost one penny. In truth they can be either cheap or expensive but are usually somewhere between £10 and £10,000.

We've also been told to say some music producers do have showers sometimes and that we're very sorry for suggesting some don't. Apologies also for lying about my height. I'm only six foot two, which is fairly tall unless you're usually standing next to a genuine giant like Greg Davies.

The other lie in this chapter is that you have to go to Chapter 7 to learn more about writing your own songs. Not really! That's Chapter 8! Instead, the next one is all about mushrooms.

Not really! That's a bonus lie. It's about farting again.

Not really! We're not allowed.

We're not going to tell you what the next chapter is about. You're just going to have to somehow turn over the page to find out. Good luck!

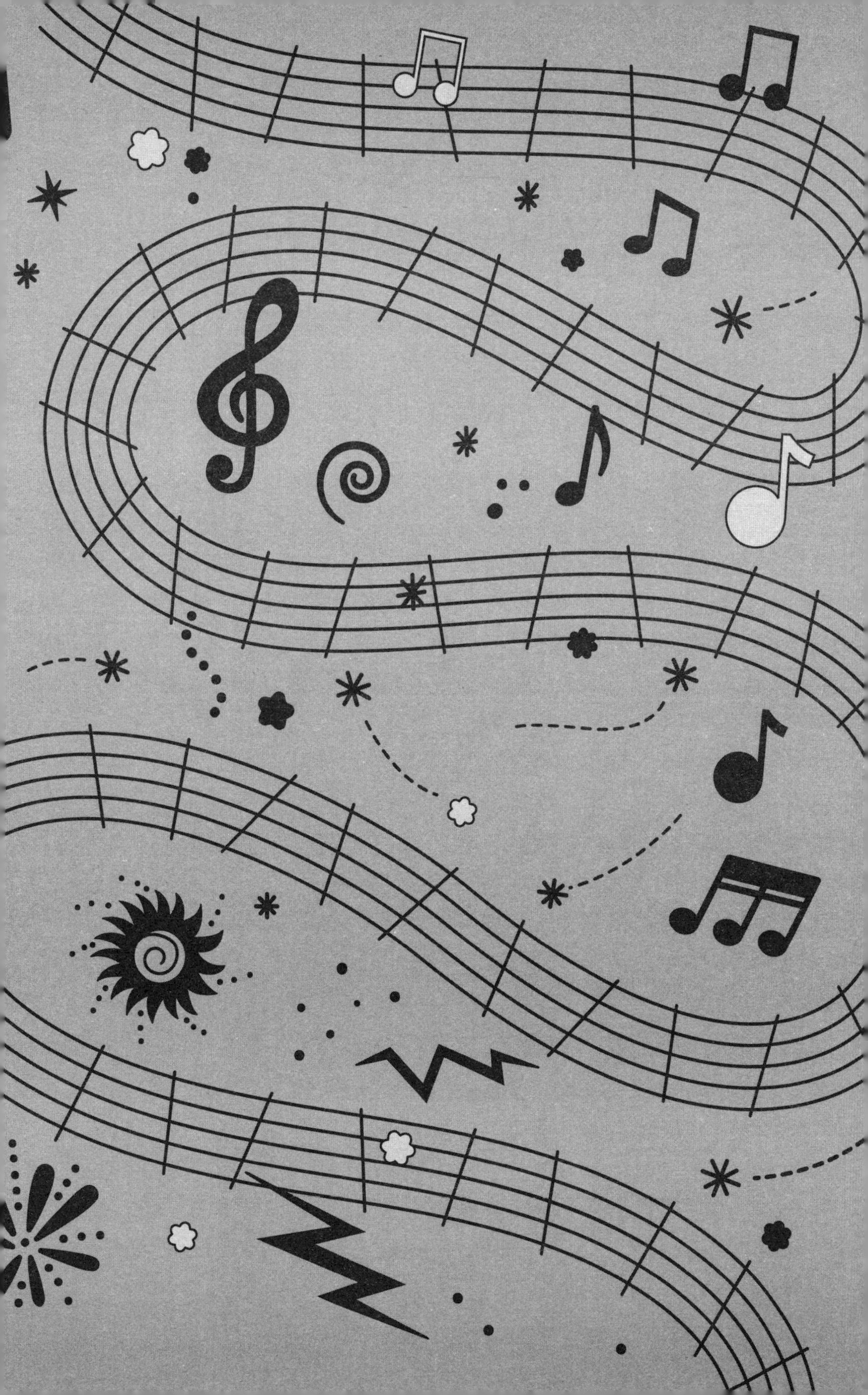

CHAPTER

SEVEN

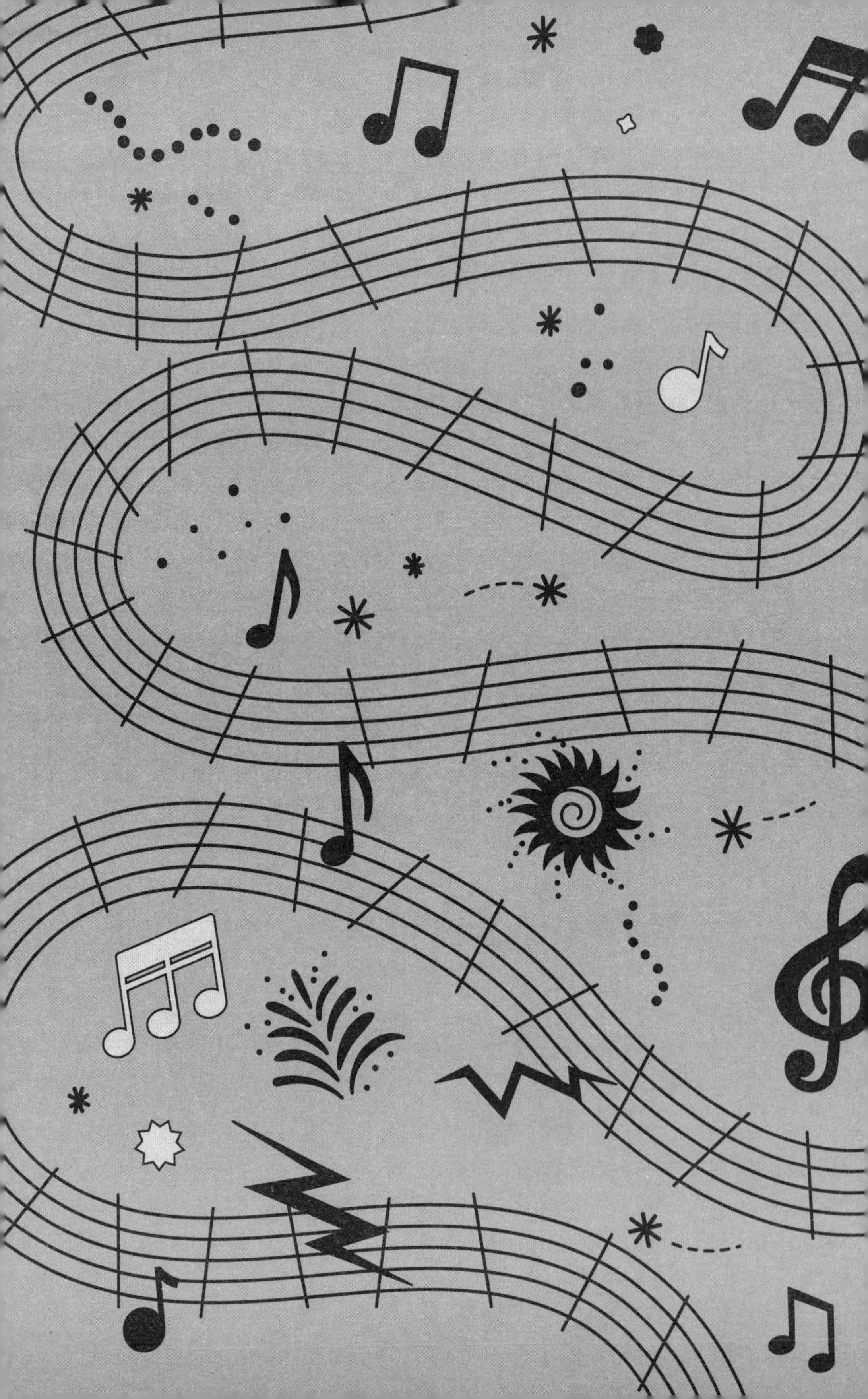

THE MUSIC RECORD BREAKERS

Hi again. Alex here still. This is my favourite chapter, so make sure you're comfortable and ready to have your mind blown. I've told you all about music and how to make it, and now it's time I answered the really serious questions:

- Which is the best song of all time?
- How do you become the best person in the world at music?
- Who is the current musical **GOAT**?
- And are there any actual musical goats?

> As usual, Alex doesn't know what he's talking about. Music isn't about being the best (or being a goat). But we agree it could be fun to take a look at some musical record breakers.

HAPPY BIRTHDAY

If you really want your song to be listened to and sung by other people for ever and ever, how about writing one to celebrate the day of the year people were born?

'Happy Birthday to You' is officially the most popular and well-known song in the world. It's also the one that everyone knows all the words to, and the lyrics have been translated into at least eighteen languages – we can't even name eighteen languages!

It was written in the late nineteenth century by two sisters called Patty and Mildred Hill, who lived in Kentucky in the USA. It was originally called 'Good Morning to All'. Their hope was that teachers would sing the song to their students and the students would sing it back. But the song was so catchy it all got a bit out of control.

When the lyrics and music were written in a book, the publisher of that book officially owned the song. A big company called Warner/Chappell Music then bought the group who had published the book, and they made people pay money every time the song was written down or sung in public. It's estimated that the song has now made more money than every song ever written, and was making over £1.6 million every year until 2016 when, after a lot of arguing, it was decided that no one actually owned 'Happy Birthday to You'.

When someone writes a song, they have something called 'copyright' of it, which means they own it. This copyright lasts for the lifetime of the author plus another seventy years. Patty died in 1946, meaning that on 1 January 2017, her song *officially* belonged to no one, and you can now sing it whenever you want. For free!

Other people have released birthday-related records; we already know about The Beatles, but have you heard their song 'Birthday'? Have a listen on your next big day. Stevie Wonder is an amazing American singer-songwriter who has played all sorts of music during his long career, and you may well have heard his song 'Happy Birthday', which is a whole lot funkier than Patty and Mildred's tune. More recently, Beyoncé's previous band, Destiny's Child, also had a pretty successful track which was simply called 'Birthday'. Yet despite these brilliant birthday songs, we all keep singing Patty and Mildred's song from 150 years ago.

Stevie Wonder is a record-breaker himself. His song 'Fingertips' was a number one in America in 1963, which, at the age of thirteen, made him the youngest-ever number-one artist.

> If you're reading this and you're not thirteen yet, get writing. If you're reading this and you're over thirteen, don't worry, there are plenty more records to break. If you're not reading this and you're over thirteen, then I can say whatever I want about you and you won't know. You're a potato, for instance. A big, muddy, slightly mouldy potato.

POTATO

The Horne Section nearly beat this record in 1992 when our first ever song, 'Le Bateau est un Chapeau', spent a month at the top of the French Pop Charts. Unfortunately we were all fourteen years old, so missed the record by a single year. If you don't do French at school, 'Le Bateau est un Chapeau' means 'The Boat is a Hat'. It's a pretty good name for a song, we think.

Christmas is another occasion when people sing the same songs over and over again. In fact, there are more songs about Christmas than anything else. Mariah Carey's 'All I Want For Christmas Is You' is still breaking records, including recently becoming the most streamed track on Spotify in a single day.

BANG-BANG WORLD RECORDS

Playing the drums is something you can do right now. Yes, RIGHT NOW. Hit something with something. Go on! There! You're playing the drums.

> Hi, everyone, it's me, Ben, an actual drummer. Just to say that they're right: if you are hitting a pan with a stick, then you are drumming. But I like to think that being an actual drummer is a bit more complicated than that. Because when I drum I actually have two sticks. So yeah. I just wanted to say that. Carry on!

There are plenty of rhythmical record-breakers out there. The world's fastest drummer is an Australian called Pritish A. R. Pritish has his own YouTube channel where he plays along to all sorts of songs. He was just eleven years old when he set his first world record: hitting a drum 2,370 times in one minute. That's 39.5 beats every single second.

That's really, really fast (although a hummingbird can beat its wings 200 times a second, so once they learn how to grip sticks, Pritish might be in trouble).

Your parents might not thank you for it, but everyone should experiment with drumming. Pritish used to whack his toys with sticks as a toddler, then played his first real drum when he was five. Now he's in the Guinness Book of Records and, more importantly, in *this* incredible book.

A team of drummers in a town called Dereham in Norfolk, UK, once drummed continuously for three days, eight hours and two minutes in August 2016, giving them the world record for the longest drumming by a team.

> And a man called Steve Gaul from Canada drummed all by himself for 121 hours (though I'm pretty sure he had to stop to go the toilet at some point).

If you want to get a world record, or if you just want to annoy your teachers, how about trying to achieve the world's longest drum roll? No, this doesn't involve taking a drum to the top of a mountain and pushing it off the top. It's when you beat a drum quickly and continuously and it makes that noise you hear just before someone reads out a big important result – such as a drum roll world record attempt.

If you want to beat the current world record for this, all you've got to do is make that noise for sixteen hours, forty-one minutes and fifty-one seconds. That'll beat Pandit Sudarshan Das by one second! He trained for an entire year for his attempt, which was to mark Queen Elizabeth's platinum jubilee (a celebration of her being the queen for seventy years).

He also played an instrument called the Indian hand tabla for 557 hours and 11 minutes, which is over twenty-five days. The hand tabla is actually a set of two different-sized drums. It's a bit like the bongos and can be fairly loud. His neighbours must be so pleased for him...

MANY MUSICIANS WITH MASSIVE INSTRUMENTS

If you don't have a spare month, then there are quicker records you could try to break. How about you get everyone in your school to play a piano at the same time? The world record was set in Birmingham in 2019, when eighty-eight school kids played just one piano. Surely you can beat that?

Well, maybe that's not as easy as it sounds. There are eighty-eight keys on a piano but actually getting eighty-eight people to squeeze round one and reach those keys is a challenge.

To set this record, engineers from Cambridge University had to design special machines to make sure everyone could reach the instrument. There were popping balloons, Hot Wheels cars, flying rabbits and nodding unicorns. The whole contraption looked like something from *Charlie and the Chocolate Factory*, with playful 'finger extenders', which allowed each child to play a note seven metres away from the piano. So you'd have to be extremely inventive to beat this record, and you'd probably need to start by inventing a piano with eighty-nine keys.

Speaking of massive contraptions, the world's biggest harp is twenty-eight metres tall and nearly twenty-two metres wide. (It is half the height of the Leaning Tower of Pisa.) The longest playable trumpet is thirty-two metres long, which is about the same as four London buses. Picture a trumpet in your head for a moment. There's the small opening at one end that you blow into – this is called the mouthpiece. At the other end there's a bigger opening where the sound comes out. This is called 'the bell'. The bell on this enormous trumpet measures five metres across, so with a bit of help a giraffe could easily step inside it!

But these are both tiny compared to the largest *natural* musical instrument. This lives underground in Virginia, USA, and covers three and a half acres – which is bigger than a cricket pitch. It's not an animal or a tree, or an enormous cave-dwelling giant, but a collection of stalactites. These are hard formations that grow down from the roof of a cave as water drips through cracks from above. They look a bit like icicles and can be just as delicate. A scientist with a brilliant name – Mr Sprinkle – managed to record the sounds of hundreds of these stalactites being carefully struck by a mallet, landing him the record for World's Largest Instrument. Well done, Mr Sprinkle.

Sounds quite tricky to play. But the hardest instrument of them all is quite clearly the conductor's baton. It doesn't come with instructions, there are no holes to blow into and no strings to twang. You just have to learn how to wave it around in exactly the right way to make the beautiful music come out. It can take years to perfect baton playing. Or you might just get lucky like me. I've never trained or practised or even thought about baton playing very much; I just swish it around and the music happens. I'm a natural.

But even I might struggle with the world's biggest baton, which was very recently made in the USA. The American Googler Orchestra used this monstrous stick to conduct a piece of music by the composer Jacques Offenbach which you have probably heard somewhere before. It's often called the Can-Can and as the stick was 4.92 metres long, it meant the conductor could-could pretty much poke any musician he wanted (which sounds to me like a great way of telling them when to play and when to be quiet!).

BIGGEST HANDS AND MARCHING BANDS

If you did have a nearly five-metre-long baton it would probably help to have enormous hands. In fact, having huge hands might help you play all these massive instruments.

The Russian pianist Sergei Rachmaninoff had some of the biggest hands in the business. He played the piano and conducted musicians at the end of the 1800s and the start of the 1900s. His hands were so large and flexible that he could play almost any piece of music brilliantly (he was also quite musical, which probably helped). These massive paddles meant some of the music composed by Rachmaninoff is almost impossible to play if you are someone with smaller than average hands. His fingers could stretch out across twelve piano keys at once. That's about a foot. Which is normally much bigger than a hand. Otherwise it would be called a hand. So his hand was about the same as a foot. Put your own hand next to your foot to see how big that is.

Now that your hand is next to your foot, let's think about walking. In fact, let's think about the most rhythmical sort of walking: marching!

Marching bands are an interesting concept. They're like normal bands, except they march. If you want to watch a marching band, you can't just sit still, otherwise you'll only see them for a few seconds. To properly enjoy them, you've got to march too. So if your favourite band happened to be a marching band, you'd get very fit watching them on tour.

Some marching bands march faster than others. In 2015 in the UK the British Imperial Marching Band marched around a swimming pool in Southampton enough times to complete a mile. They did this in fourteen minutes and twenty-six seconds, which means their pace was somewhere between a fast walk and a jog. This is impressive considering they were all carrying instruments, and even more impressive when you find out they did it while on board a cruise ship.

> I'm quite glad the band I conduct doesn't move around. It's hard enough keeping control of them when they're all sitting down. If they were constantly wandering around, I wouldn't know where to point my stick.

Alex should also be glad there are only five other musicians in the band. The largest marching band in the world had a total of 11,157 people involved. They marched about in Osaka, Japan, in 1997, to celebrate the sixtieth anniversary of something called the Music for Wind Instruments League. This is an organization that gets like-minded musicians together, and this particular marching group was made up of 317 bands. That's a very noisy walk.

There was another huge band called So Solid Crew who in the early 2000s had thirty members. They played a type of music called UK garage, as well as hip hop, and produced quite serious-sounding dance music. Not all the band members played actual instruments, most were MCs that rapped over the music, but all played a part in what was a really popular (if quite impractical) act. But that's tiny compared to the American hip hop group Minority Militia. They have 124 members who all contributed to their album *The People's Army* in 2001.

> Six people in a comedy music group is also quite a lot. It means that any money we earn is split between us and, more importantly, any snacks that come our way don't last long.

BONUS RANDOM RECORDS

Do you want to guess the fewest number of notes in a piece of classical music? Go on then.

Unless you said zero, you were wrong. A piece of music called 4'33" was 'written' by the composer John Cage and has no notes at all. It's four minutes and thirty-three seconds of silence and can apparently be played on 'any instrument'. You can see the piece being performed by a full orchestra on the internet. There's even a conductor with his baton and an audience applauding. All the musicians stand and bow at the end, which is probably fair enough. After all, they didn't play a single wrong note.

What's most interesting is that there is actually no silence during the performance. Even when the musicians aren't playing their instruments there's the buzz of people being in a room together; there's coughing, laughing, the ruffling of clothes and the turning of pages by the conductor. If it was much more than four and a half minutes, it might get boring, but we recommend you give it a try yourself. (You could even choose it for the first dance at your wedding.)

Cage himself said, 'Everything we do is music,' and we completely agree. Banging a pan with a stick *is* music! You are a musician! Everyone can play music!

The opposite of a full orchestra playing no music is probably one person playing all the music. This is called a one-man band and they are always good fun to watch. You don't have to be a man though, anyone can be a one-man band!

Rory Blackwell gained the world record for the biggest one-man band when he played 108 different instruments at the same time in Devon on 29 May 1989. His one-person orchestra was made up of eighty-nine percussion instruments and nineteen melodic ones. The beater he used to strike his drums had twenty-two prongs so he could play loads of drums at the same time, which made quite a racket.

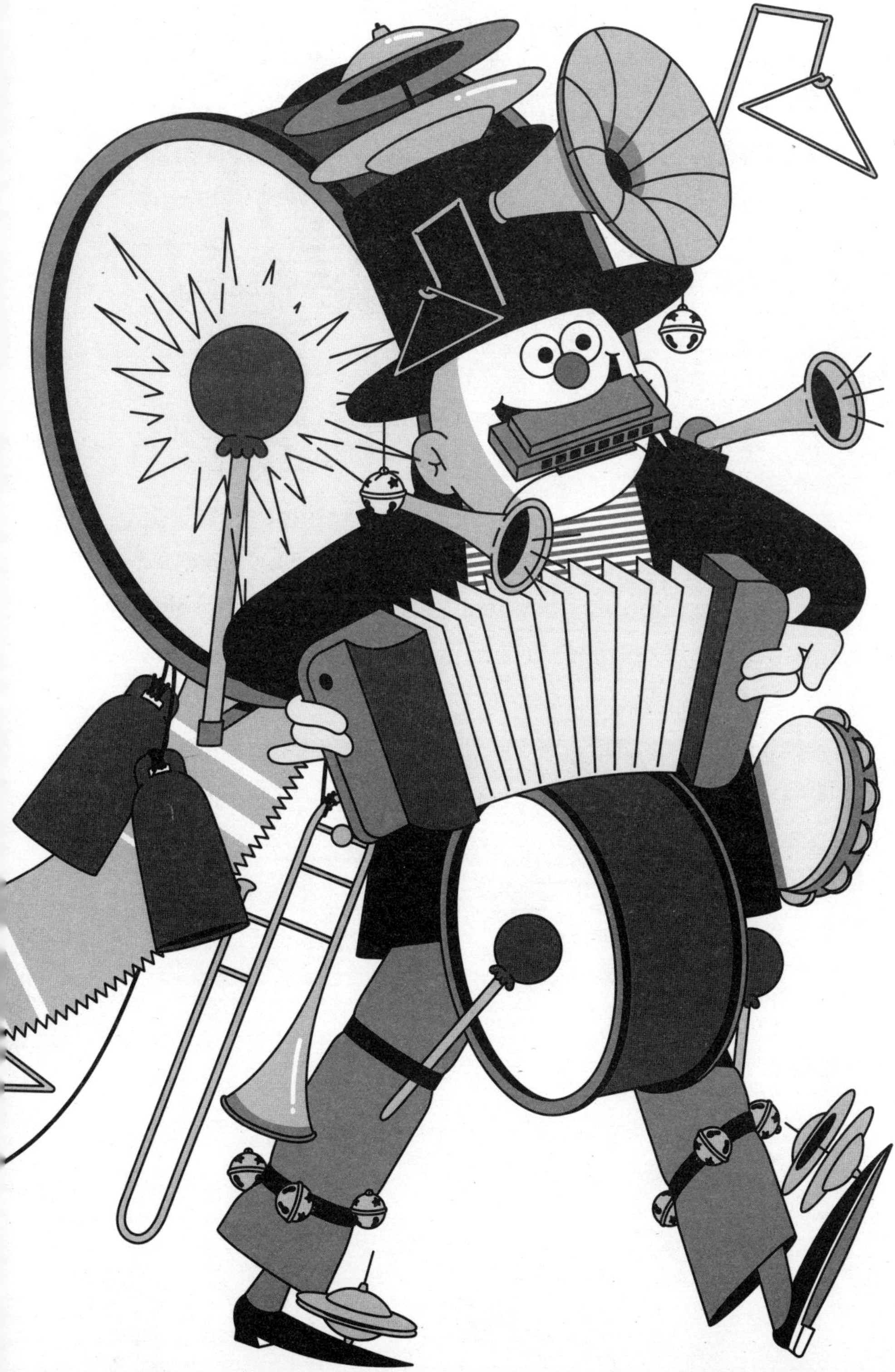

BAND CHAT

Band: So that's the end of this musical world record chapter. We hope we have inspired you to try to break a musical record, either with your friends or all by yourself.

Alex: Sorry, you can't end it here. It's all very well talking all about the longest instruments and the biggest bands, but what about goats? I want to know about the musical goats!

Band: Really?

Alex: Really.

Band: Fine. Well, there are indeed plenty of musical goats. There's one called Pickle Butt, who you can see playing some wind chimes with his head. There's one rhythmically bashing a metal fence with his horns. Swiss Alps goats wear bells round their necks. And there's one on YouTube listening to music with headphones and dancing. Sort of.

It all goes to show that whether you're a thirteen-year-old, a person with giant hands or a goat on a mountain in Switzerland, there's no excuse. Get playing music. It really is for everyone.

ALEX HAS LEFT THE CONVERSATION.

MUSICAL TASKS

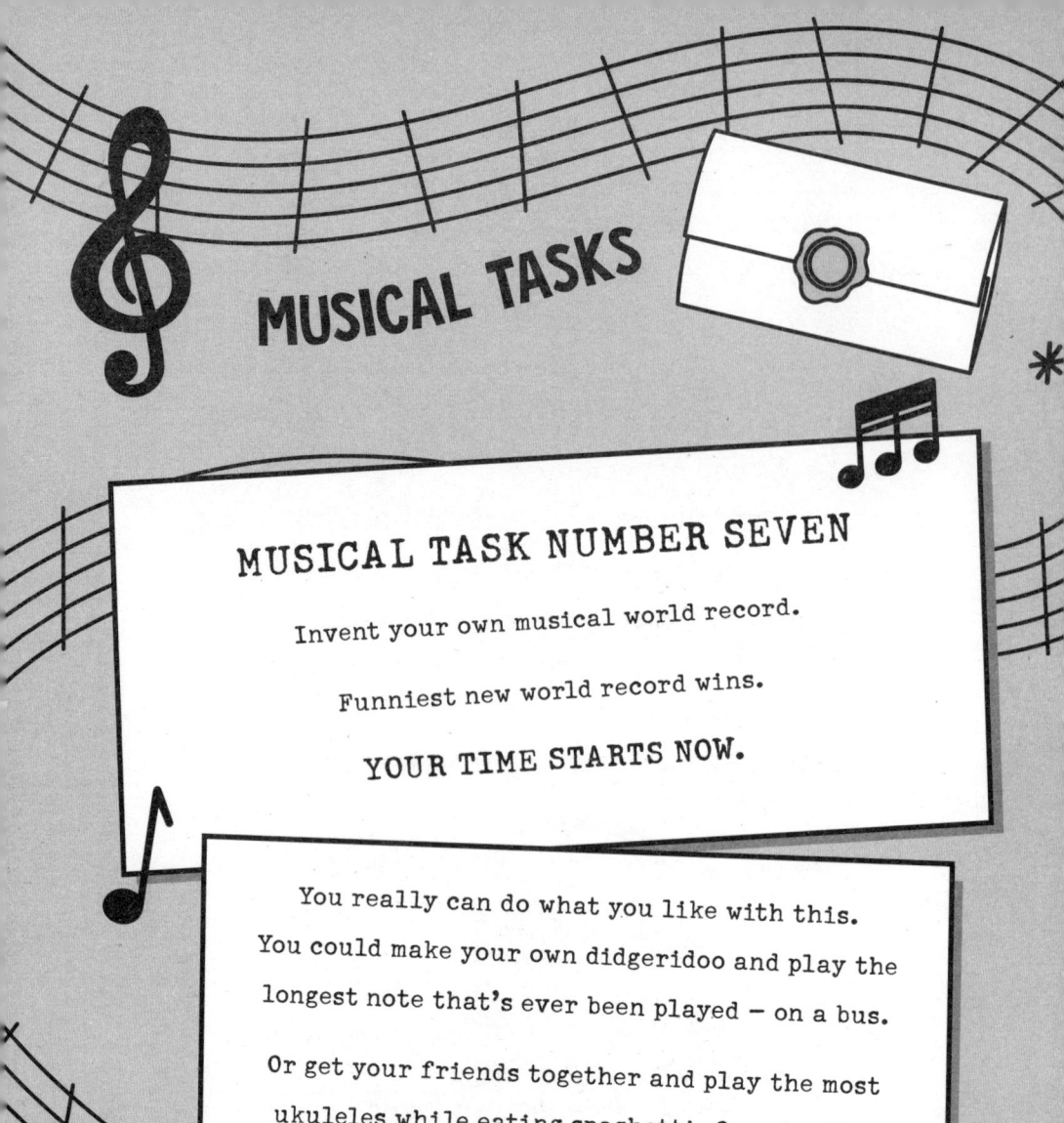

MUSICAL TASK NUMBER SEVEN

Invent your own musical world record.

Funniest new world record wins.

YOUR TIME STARTS NOW.

You really can do what you like with this. You could make your own didgeridoo and play the longest note that's ever been played — on a bus.

Or get your friends together and play the most ukuleles while eating spaghetti. Or actually roll a drum down a mountain to set a different type of drum roll record. (actually, we strongly recommend that you *don't* do that . . .)

The possibilities are endless and your time has already started.

THE LIES!

Unfortunately we haven't written a song called 'Le Bateau est un Chapeau' and we've never topped any musical charts anywhere in the world. We would love to listen to a song called 'Le Bateau est un Chapeau', though, so why not write it yourself? The title already rhymes and there are so many interesting questions. Why is the boat a hat? Who is wearing the boat? Are they getting wet? Please do share your results. Who knows, maybe you'll top the charts with it one day. And if you can persuade your whole school to sing it at sports day, while running round the sports field, you'll definitely get a handful of world records too.

There's a subtle lie in the marching bands section. You don't have to march next to a marching band to enjoy the marching band. Marching bands also march around fields and stadiums, and they are amazing things to watch. They're particularly popular in America where most schools now have marching bands.

We should also explain that there aren't more songs about Christmas than anything else. Most songs are actually about things like breaking up with someone or not wanting to break up with someone or kissing someone. Yuck.

CHAPTER

EIGHT

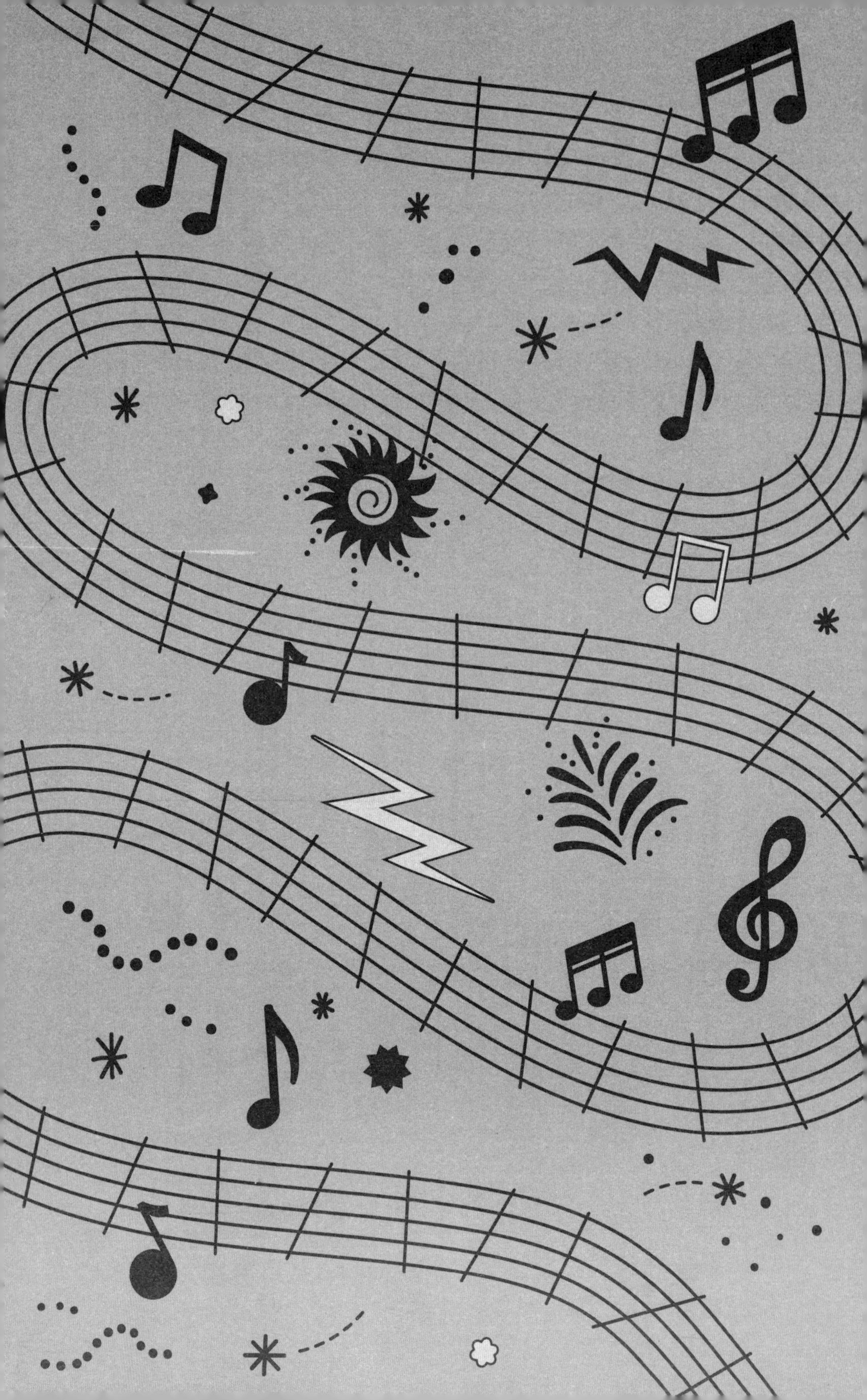

CAN WE WRITE A SONG NOW?

When you've finished reading this book (or maybe even when you've finished reading this sentence), I want you to write a song.

If you've not written a song yet, that's OK! Simply read on.

Songs shouldn't be things that just other people write. You should think of them like pictures. Anyone can paint a picture and stick it up on their fridge. Similarly everyone can write a song and sing it to their family over breakfast. It might not be any good – and that's totally fine, you just need to keep at it. But it *might* be really good. (And everyone will almost certainly say they like it.)

There are about 100 million songs on the streaming service Spotify and more than 60,000 new songs are uploaded every day. You can add to these numbers right now. All you've got to do is do it!

We've told you about the instruments, the writing and the recording, so you have all those tools ready to go. What you need now is an idea. One tiny flash of inspiration.

Maybe you've realized how much you like cornflakes – that could be enough to get started! Express your love for the famous breakfast cereal with some rhyming words and a cheerful tune. Scribble the words down first, then try to sing them to the first tune that comes out of your mouth. Or shut your eyes, think of pouring the milk into the bowl and on to the crispy flakes, and hum whatever pops into your brain.

The most important thing is that you jot down all your ideas and keep trying to turn them into something tuneful. It might not be perfect right away but it'll be the start of something and that something might just be brilliant.

OUR FAVOURITE SONGWRITERS

The Horne Section write our own songs. We have written nearly 250 and every single one is exceptional. But just occasionally we listen to songs written by other people.

Irving Berlin, an American composer (and someone many people regard as the greatest songwriter of all time), wrote around 1,500 songs. BUT he lived for 101 years so that's only about one a month. The Horne Section are coming for you, Irving!

More people have listened to Irving's songs than ours, though (so far). Do you know the song 'White Christmas'? It has sold 50 million records. You know the one – you probably hear it on the radio every year.

But while it was sung by Bing Crosby, can you take a guess at who wrote it?

IRVING BERLIN!

It has since been recorded by 500 different artists, including smooth singers like Frank Sinatra and Michael Bublé, legends such as Elvis Presley, and 1960s Motown group the Supremes. Even modern pop stars like Jessie J and Lady Gaga have had a go. The song has combined sales of over 100 million records. Personally we're dreaming of writing the next 'White Christmas'.

So songwriters don't have to be singers, and singers don't have to be songwriters. Elvis recorded over 800 songs but wrote zero songs himself. Pop icon Rihanna only came up with a few of the tunes she's recorded, and the hugely famous singers Celine Dion and Whitney Houston have always tended to belt out other people's music.

Paul McCartney writes and sings and is almost certainly the most successful British songwriter – he's written or co-written over 500 songs (and counting). You probably know him from his band The Beatles, whose songs were nearly all written by him and John Lennon. He also co-wrote with many other great songwriters, including Stevie Wonder. In total Paul has had twenty-two number ones in the UK and thirty-two in the USA, winning eighteen Grammys in the process!

Then you also get people like the great Max Martin. You've not heard of Max? That's probably because the twenty-five US number-one songs he's written were all given to other people to sing. Huge pop stars like Britney Spears, Katy Perry, Taylor Swift, Kelly Clarkson, Justin Timberlake and The Weeknd have all topped the charts thanks to Max, as have groups including NSYNC, Maroon 5 and BTS.

BAND CHAT

Alex: So how can kids become the next Max Martin?

Band: If we knew that, we wouldn't be messing around writing silly books.

Alex: Good point. Then how can kids become the next Horne Section?

Band: You mess around a lot and eventually write a silly book. But, first things first, you write some songs. And as we are a comedy band, our job is to create songs that make people laugh. Here's a song about how we write songs – and how you can write one too.

It's called 'Ding Ding' and instead of reading it, why not sing it out loud? You can invent a tune or use one that already exists ('Jingles Bells' just about works).

DING DING

FIRST THE VERSE, SET THE SCENE,
YOU CAN TAKE YOUR TIME.

GET THE LISTENER INTERESTED,
SOME OF IT COULD RHYME.

BEGIN TO PAINT THE PICTURE,
TELL THE STORY OF THE SONG,

THEN GET ON WITH THE CHORUS –
IT'S TIME TO SING ALONG.

NOW WE'RE AT THE CHORUS.

YOU CANNOT IGNORE US.

GET READY TO SING:

DING, DING, DING, DING, DING.

WE ALL LOVE THE CHORUS.

HERE YOU MUST NOT BORE US.

IT'S TIME TO JOIN IN:

DING, DING, DING, DING, DING.

WE'RE DOING PRETTY WELL –
WE'VE REACHED THE SECOND VERSE.

EVERY VERSE IS MUSICALLY THE SAME AS THE FIRST,

BUT THE STORY'S MOVING ON AND WE'RE
HAVING FUN WITH WORDS.

PLEASE DON'T GIVE IT ALL AWAY –
SAVE SOMETHING FOR THE THIRD.

NOW WE'RE AT THE CHORUS.

YOU CANNOT IGNORE US.

GET READY TO SING:

DING, DING, DING, DING, DING.

WE ALL LOVE THE CHORUS.

HERE YOU MUST NOT BORE US.

IT'S TIME TO JOIN IN:

DING, DING, DING, DING, DING.

A LOT OF PEOPLE DO NOT HAVE A
GREAT ATTENTION SPAN,

SO GET THE STORY WRAPPED UP IN
THREE VERSES IF YOU CAN.

IF YOUR SONG'S A MASSIVE HIT OR
PEOPLE FIND IT FUNNY,

PLEASE REMEMBER US AND SEND US
ROUGHLY HALF THE MONEY.

NOW WE'RE AT THE CHORUS.
YOU CANNOT IGNORE US.
GET READY TO SING:
DING, DING, DING, DING, DING.

WE ALL LOVE THE CHORUS.

HERE YOU MUST NOT BORE US.

IT'S TIME TO JOIN IN:

DING, DING, DING, DING, DING.

WHAT MAKES A SONG?

Just in case 'Ding Ding' didn't give you all the instructions you need to make a song, let's have a closer look at all the different elements.

You might still be wondering where to actually start. And the answer is – there is no right place to start! You could have a go at writing some words to a song you already know well. Or you could write a new tune for some existing words. See which you prefer. Some people come up with a melody first and add the words much later; others just have a sentence they can't stop singing and this eventually grows into a whole piece of music.

Wherever you end up starting, here are the names of all the different parts of a song, so you'll at least know what you're aiming for.

THE HOOK

The 'ding ding ding ding' line is what we call the hook. It's the bit that catches your ear, stays in your head and that you'll be singing forever. It has to be simple, snappy and easy to remember. A brilliant hook could end up being sung by people all around the world.

Here are some songs with the hookiest hooks, so catchy they are probably already living in your head without you even knowing:

'WE WILL ROCK YOU' BY QUEEN

'SINGLE LADIES' BY BEYONCÉ

'HAPPY' BY PHARRELL WILLIAMS

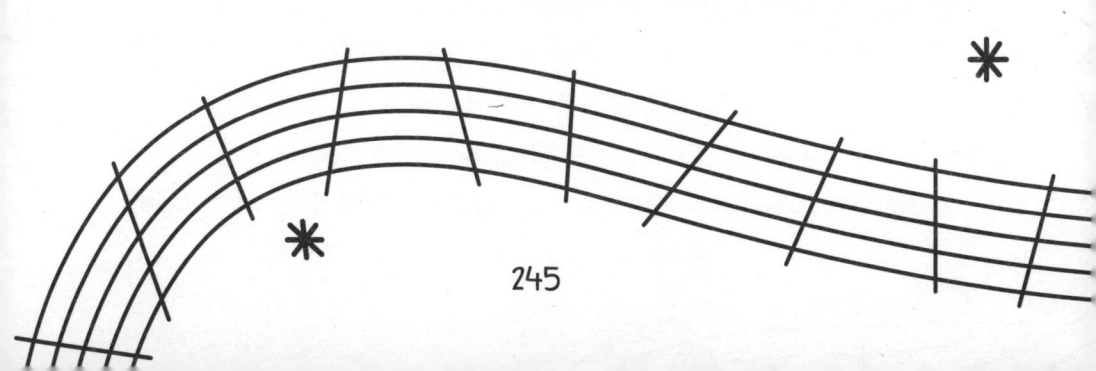

THE MELODY

The melody is really another word for the tune. It's the combination of notes that makes a song sound like it does. The melody will give your music its flavour: happy, sad, thoughtful, playful or whatever you want it to feel like. It's perhaps the most important part of a song because a catchy melody will stick in people's heads.

But surely all combinations of notes have already been tried? Luckily, even with just eight notes to play with, there are billions of possible tunes to be made, and that's before you start mucking about with long notes and short notes, funky rhythms and different harmonies.

If you have a keyboard or piano you can have a play, pressing the keys until you've made something you like the sound of. Or you could just hum whatever pops into your head. Once again, there's no right or wrong way.

Some people, like the great British singer and pianist Elton John, have a special talent for coming up with melodies. And sometimes these tuneful folk have other people they turn to for writing the words. A man called Bernie Taupin wrote nearly all the lyrics for Elton's songs, for example. Similarly in the world of musicals there's often a composer who writes the music and a lyricist who writes what they call 'the book' - the words. Elton John actually wrote the music for *The Lion King*, for example, while a writer called

Tim Rice came up with all the words (Tim did the same with Andrew Lloyd Webber for *Joseph and the Amazing Technicolor Dreamcoat* and *Jesus Christ Superstar*). If you're lucky enough to have a band, everyone can chip in – and you might just end up with a smash hit.

Paul McCartney is a unique songwriter, and he wrote a song called 'Yesterday' in a very strange way. He woke up one morning with the melody for the song already in his head. Unfortunately he hadn't come up with the words yet. So before he'd even eaten his breakfast he hurriedly wrote some lyrics so he didn't forget the tune. If you don't know the song already, ask someone to play it for you. Then try singing these words to the same tune:

> Scrambled eggs, oh, my baby, how I love your legs, Not as much as I love scrambled eggs.

THE BRIDGE

You could also add a bridge to your song. This section normally sounds different to the rest of the song and only appears once, often between the final verse and chorus. It can provide what we call 'contrast', which means it offers something a bit different, surprising the listener and sometimes changing the tone of the song. Unlike the repeated chorus, the words and music are both new and fresh. If you need a bit more time to get the story of your song across, a bridge can be really helpful.

'Oops!...I Did It Again' by Britney Spears is a good example of a bridge. Put it on and see if you can spot this section.

If you're not sure, listen out after the second chorus. Just when you think you know where the song is going, there's a huge difference in the music, the singing becomes talking, the melody changes and the song shifts to a new place.

Unlike Britney, we in the Horne Section are experts in writing silly songs. Ideally these will make you laugh, and if not, they should at least be slightly amusing. We think it's much harder to write a funny song than a sad song, but we do have a few comedy secrets up our sleeves. Most of our songs fall into one of three different categories so you could have a crack at any one of these.

> Well, a bridge is really helpful if you need to get across anything.

DUM-DUM SONGS

Nonsense songs! These are songs that don't mean anything to us or anyone else. They are a total waste of everybody's time and therefore the best use of everybody's time. They're often fairly short, rarely much longer than a minute. Sometimes they're just words that don't seem to make sense. Sometimes they tell a silly story.

Our ultimate dum-dum song is called 'Thick and Creamy' and has only one line (though if you keep repeating this line, the song can last for up to eight minutes):

THICK AND CREAMY, THAT'S HOW I LIKE MY MILK.

We've also got a much shorter one all about the recent pandemic. It goes like this:

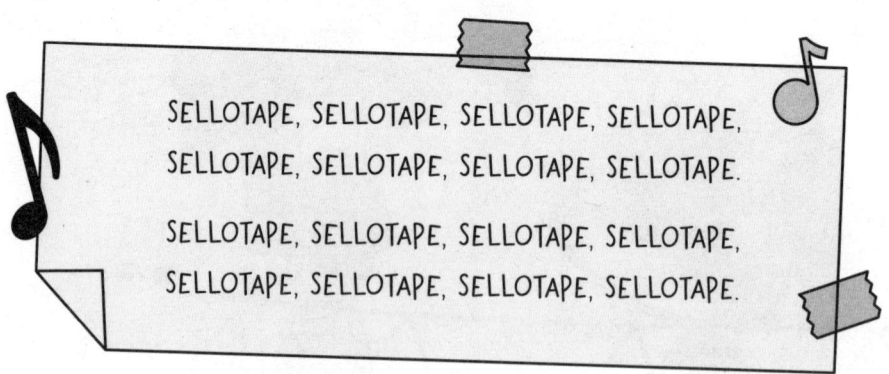

SELLOTAPE, SELLOTAPE, SELLOTAPE, SELLOTAPE,
SELLOTAPE, SELLOTAPE, SELLOTAPE, SELLOTAPE.

SELLOTAPE, SELLOTAPE, SELLOTAPE, SELLOTAPE,
SELLOTAPE, SELLOTAPE, SELLOTAPE, SELLOTAPE.

That one's called 'Sticky Situation'.

Songs that tell a story can be a bit longer. Here's the beginning of one of ours, about the Olympic gold-medal-winning cyclist Chris Hoy:

CHRIS HOY

VERSE 1

OLD CHRIS HOY ATE A JUMBO SAVELOY
ON THE MORNING OF A RACE.

IT DIDN'T HELP AT ALL, HE BROKE THE GOLDEN RULE,
AND HE FINISHED IN LAST PLACE.

THE NEXT TIME HE COMPETED YET AGAIN HE PUT THE MEAT
IN, ANOTHER SAVELOY FOR HOY.

HE DECIDED THAT HIS PEDALS HAD EARNED HIM ENOUGH
MEDALS AND SAVELOYS BROUGHT MORE JOY.

CHORUS

CHRIS HOY LOVES A SAVELOY —
HE'S SUCH A NAUGHTY BOY.

HIS WIFE GETS QUITE ANNOYED.

CHRIS HOY, HOY, HOY LOVES A SAVELOY —
HE LOVES A SAVELOY.

The process for writing this song involved choosing two unrelated words that rhyme, thinking of a way of connecting those two words and writing a nonsense story around that.

Try writing a dum-dum story song. You could use the structure of 'Ding Ding' if that's a helpful starting point. Your story can be as silly as you like, about anything at all, and the rhythm and tune can be really simple. In other words, try writing a dum-dum ding-ding song.

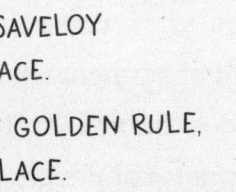

RUG-PULL SONGS

A comedy technique known as the 'rug-pull' is when you trick or surprise the audience. The name comes from the idea of someone standing on a rug that you yank out from under them. Then they fall and are left confused (which is how a lot of people feel after our shows).

Music is a really helpful tool for a rug-pull. You could use the tune to create a mood or atmosphere that doesn't match the lyrics or what the song is supposed to be about. Or you could tell a story that takes a completely unexpected turn. You could suddenly turn a sad song into a funny song. Or use a spooky melody with cheery words. The thing to remember with music is that you are controlling people's minds – and you can use this to make them laugh. Songwriters have special powers!

TIP: THE BEST PLACE TO PULL THE RUG IS IN THE CHORUS OR AT THE END.

See if you can work out where this song is going:

BEING WITH YOU

YOU TURN YOUR BACK, AND YOU WALK AWAY,
AND I AM LEFT HERE WITH NOTHING TO SAY.
YOU DON'T SEEM TO CARE ABOUT LEAVING THIS MESS.
YOU DON'T SEEM TO NOTICE MY DISTRESS.
THEN I REACH OUT, I HOLD OUT MY HAND,
I LOOK TO THE SKY AND I LOOK TO THE GROUND.
THERE'S NO GETTING ROUND WHAT I HAVE TO DO.
I GUESS IT'S JUST PART OF BEING WITH YOU.
I PICK UP YOUR POO . . .

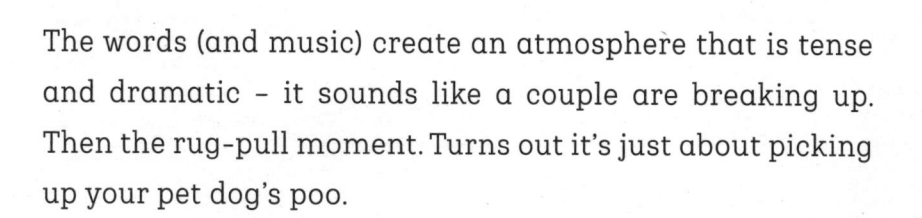

The words (and music) create an atmosphere that is tense and dramatic – it sounds like a couple are breaking up. Then the rug-pull moment. Turns out it's just about picking up your pet dog's poo.

Have you ever tricked anyone? Or has anyone tricked you? Try writing the story down in song form and see if it could have a similar rug-pull effect.

PUNS AND JOKES

Some of our songs are just jokes set to music. Turning a joke into a song is a great way to start writing funny tunes. And sometimes we try to cram in as many gags as possible. Puns (word-based jokes) are particularly useful for this. Here's the start of one such song:

'DINOSAUR'

I WOKE UP THIS MORNING AND YAWNED AND STRETCHED.

I ATE UP MY TOAST AND READY BREK.

IN THE GARDEN YOU WOULD NOT BELIEVE WHAT I SAW:

A LARGE VEGETARIAN DINOSAUR,

A DIPLODOCUS NAMED ELEANOR

AND I HAD TO ADMIT I'D NEVER SEEN HER BEFORE ... HERBIVORE.

Get it? No? Say the last line out loud. Get it now? ✱

This is just the first verse of six! You can find the lyrics to all six verses on page 276. Each verse ends with a silly pun that in some way relates to dinosaurs.

Do you have a favourite joke? Try singing it to a tune. You could even add to the beginning of the joke, stringing it out a bit for extra drama.

Having said all this, we would now like to say . . .

THERE ARE NO RULES TO SONGWRITING!

If your song sounds good or makes people feel certain emotions when they hear it, you've written a great song! If it does both, please tell us how you did it. (We don't really know what we're doing. We've also never written a book before, so the idea that we could write a book about how to write a song is completely ridiculous. Well done, Puffin!)

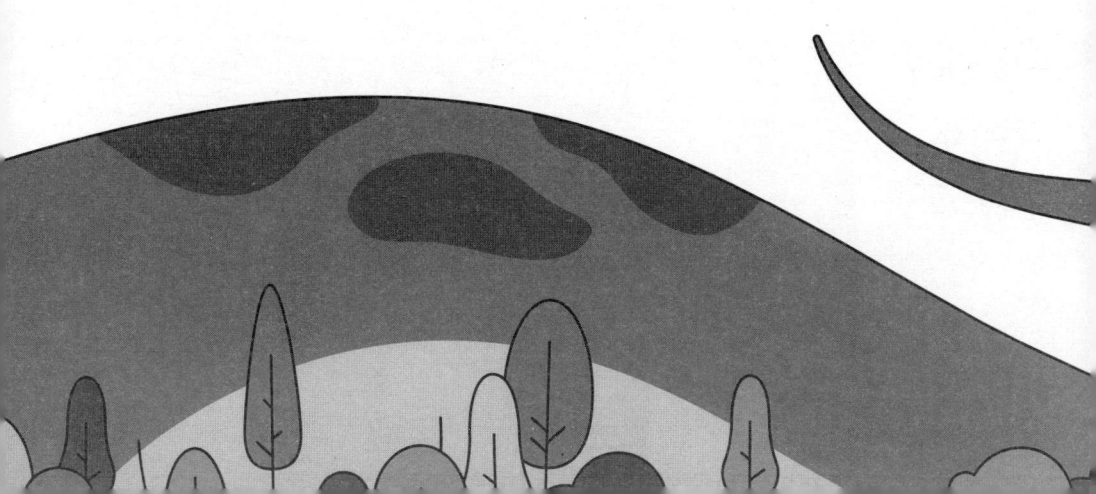

To finish the chapter, here's a conversation Joe once had with Noel Gallagher from the English rock band Oasis:

Joe: Sorry to bother you, Noel, but do you have any tips on songwriting?

Noel: Who on earth are you?

Joe: I'm the trumpeter that's been touring with you for the last five years.

Noel: Really? What's your name?

Joe: Joe.

Noel: Well, Joe, the more time you spend at the river, the more fish you catch.

Joe: Yes, but I was hoping for some tips on songwriting, Noel.

Noel: Well, Joe, the more time you spend at the river, the more fish you catch.

Unfortunately they were stood by a river, and Noel fell in, so Joe never got to ask him what he meant by this. We *think* what he's saying is that you have to do something a lot to get good at it. The more time you spend playing and writing music, the better the musician you'll become.

MUSICAL TASKS

MUSICAL TASK NUMBER EIGHT

Perform a song that starts slow, then speeds up and lasts exactly one minute.

Most satisfying speed-up song wins.

YOUR TIME STARTS NOW.

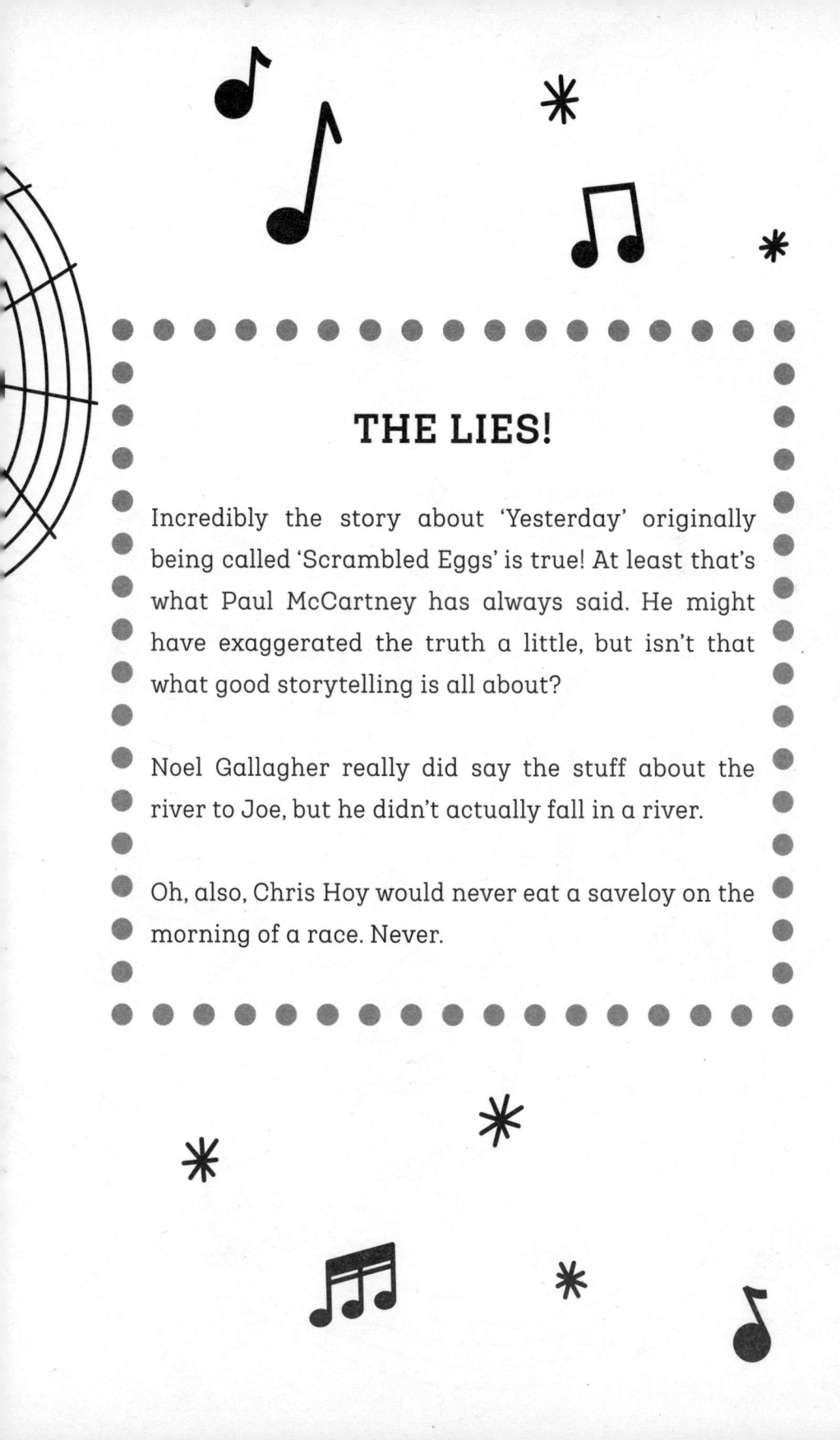

THE LIES!

Incredibly the story about 'Yesterday' originally being called 'Scrambled Eggs' is true! At least that's what Paul McCartney has always said. He might have exaggerated the truth a little, but isn't that what good storytelling is all about?

Noel Gallagher really did say the stuff about the river to Joe, but he didn't actually fall in a river.

Oh, also, Chris Hoy would never eat a saveloy on the morning of a race. Never.

CHAPTER

NINE

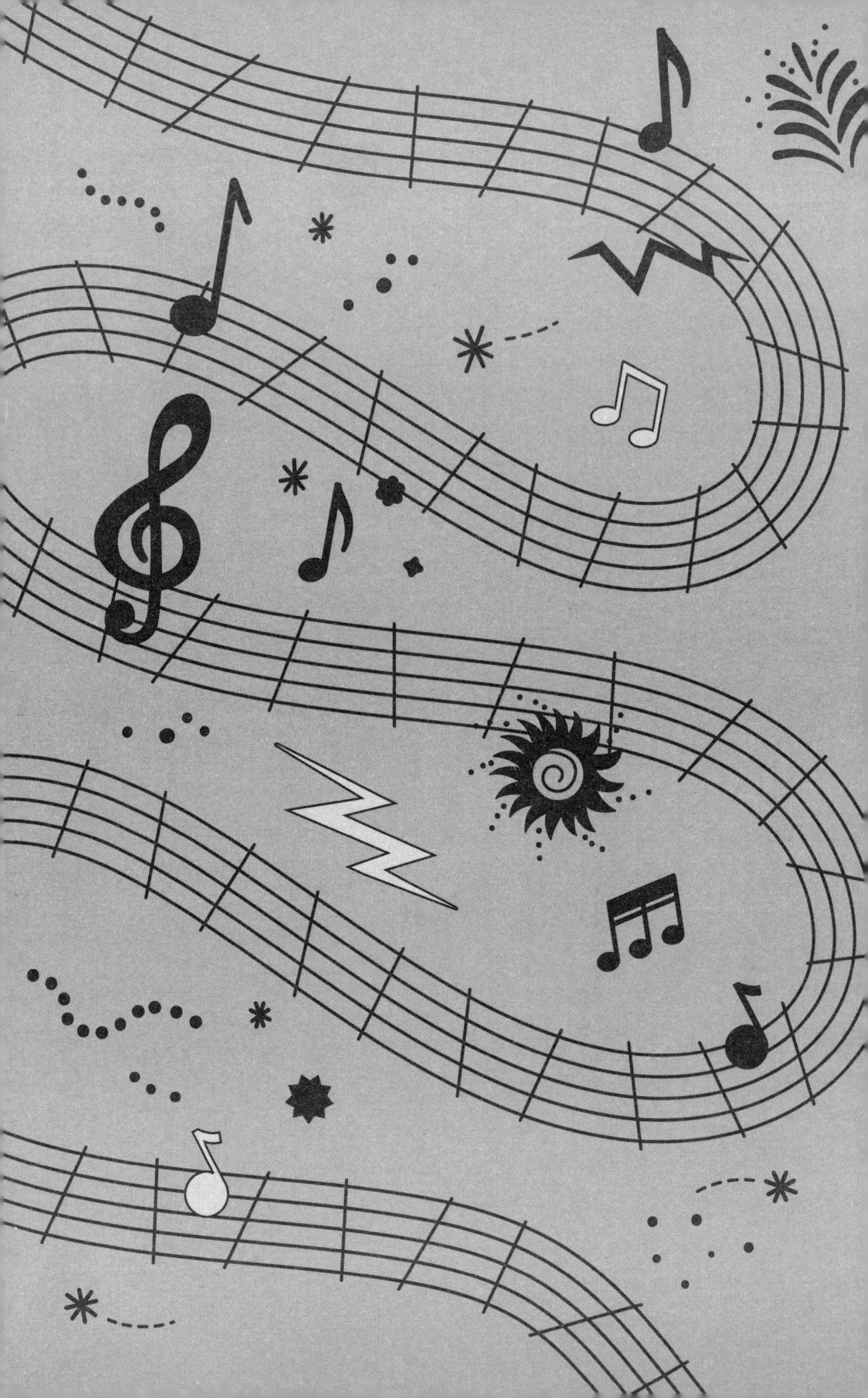

WHAT WAS ALL THAT ABOUT?

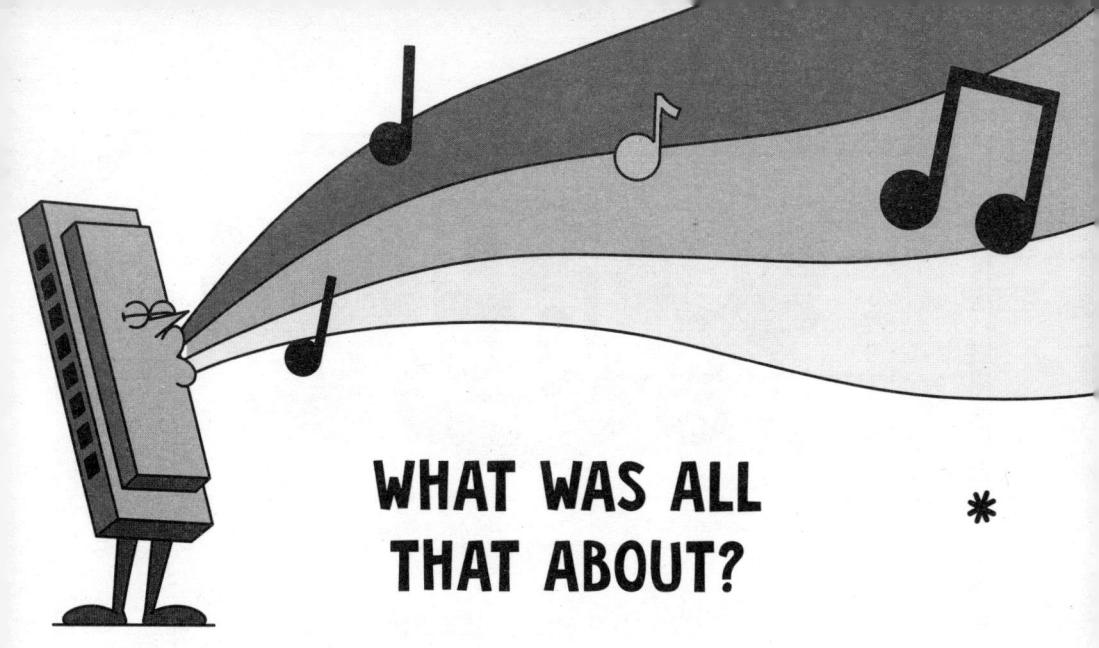

If you've managed to read this far, congratulations. You are now officially a Grade 9 musician. People might tell you the official grades only go up to eight but that's because they haven't got this far themselves. So go and grab a piece of paper and trace the certificate on the next page.

GRADE 9 MUSIC CERTIFICATE

I _____ know everything there is to know about music because I read:

MAKE SOME NOISE BY THE HORNE SECTION

and it was brilliant and I'm definitely going to either buy another five copies or tell five of my friends to buy a copy each.

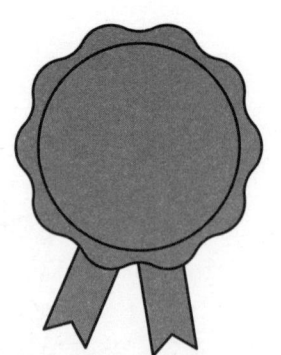

While this book has been packed with lies, we want to be honest with you now.

Being a musician or even just enjoying music isn't about grades or exams. It's not even about understanding how music works, how it's made, recorded or written down. It's about letting it into your life, making time for it and embracing everything it can do for you. It's about letting your toes tap as you listen to some gentle jazz in your grandparents' car. Letting your arms wave as your favourite pop tune plays in a park. And letting your mind feel and your body move, dance and sway to whichever songs you enjoy, wherever you are.

MUSIC IS FUN. And it is everywhere. Shut your eyes and listen to all the music going on around you. You might be able to hear the beats of a hip hop song on the radio, the natural music of birds chirruping or the rise and fall of your grandpa's snores. You could sing or drum or hum along to any of those sounds.

BAND CHAT

Band: You are the same as Alex now: music is at your fingertips. You should have all you need to go out, find it and make it.

Alex: I just wanted to say that you're not exactly the same as me. I am officially a band leader, main singer and I played the French horn to Grade 4 standard.

Band: Yes, he's right. You're not exactly the same as Alex. You are far more musical. Because Alex may have written a book, but you have read that book and that's far more impressive.

Band: Have you ever wondered why it's called 'playing' music? It's because playing music is all about mucking about, experimenting and exploring. So whether you're using a pan as a drum, a cucumber as a flute or even a real-life instrument, if you can turn practising into playing, you'll have fun and get better and better without even realizing it. When you play cricket in the park or draw a picture in your bedroom, you don't think of that as practice. But every time you do something you get better at that thing. So play alone or find a few friends, and just enjoy yourself.

We've been playing music all our lives. Ben, Joe and Alex have known each other since they were babies and are still playing together nearly half a century later. We feel so lucky that we get paid to sing songs and dance around like we did when we were kids. It's definitely more fun than lots of other jobs! And even if you can't turn it into a job, it's the best hobby out there. Cricket stops in the rain and you can't skateboard on a train. But get yourself some headphones and you can have secret music in your head all day long.

And that's it. We've told you everything we know. Now it's your turn. We can't wait to hear what new sounds you come up with, what genres of music you invent and what funny songs you create. You never know, people across the world might just be singing your song in a hundred years' time.

MUSICAL TASKS

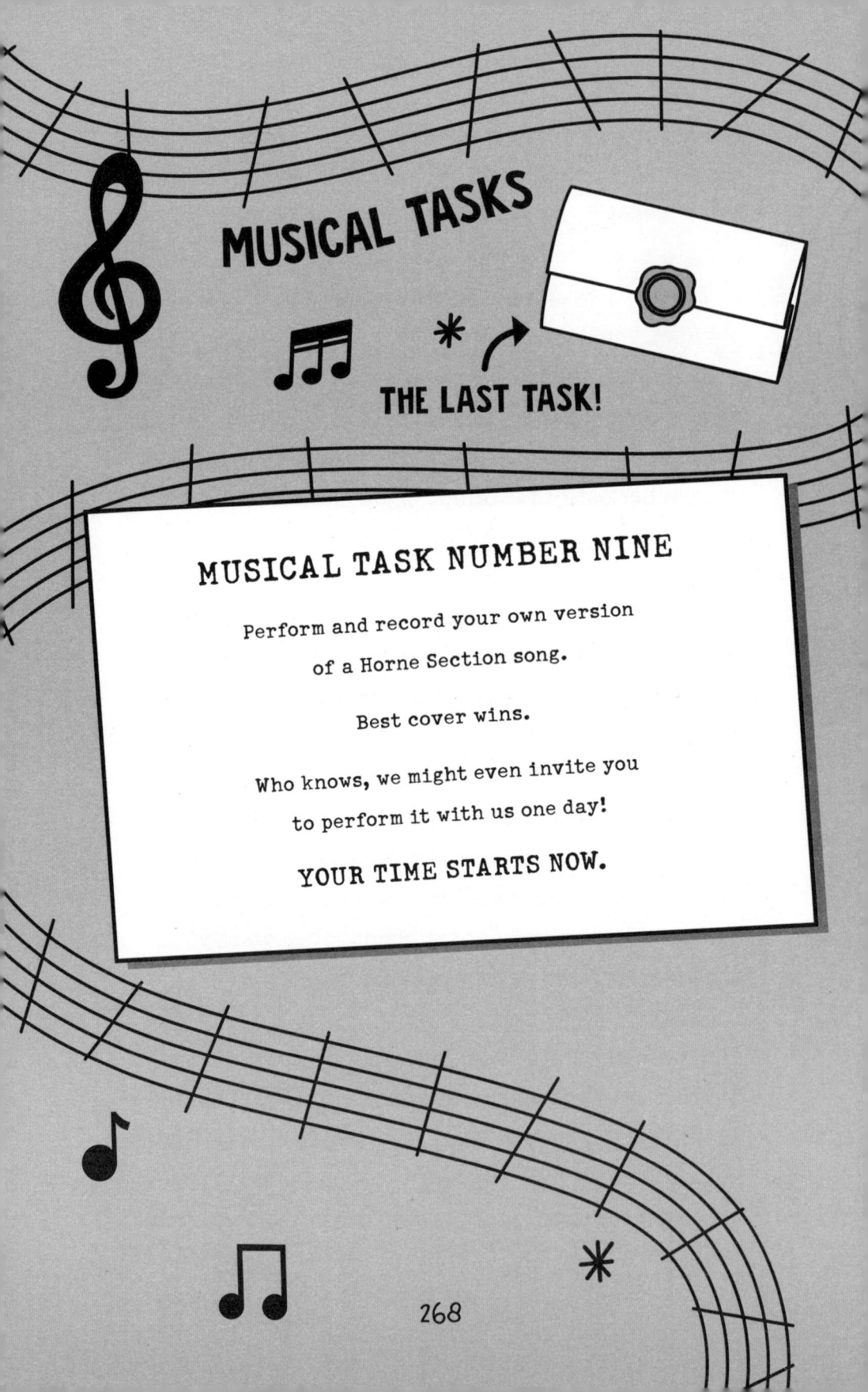

THE LAST TASK!

MUSICAL TASK NUMBER NINE

Perform and record your own version of a Horne Section song.

Best cover wins.

Who knows, we might even invite you to perform it with us one day!

YOUR TIME STARTS NOW.

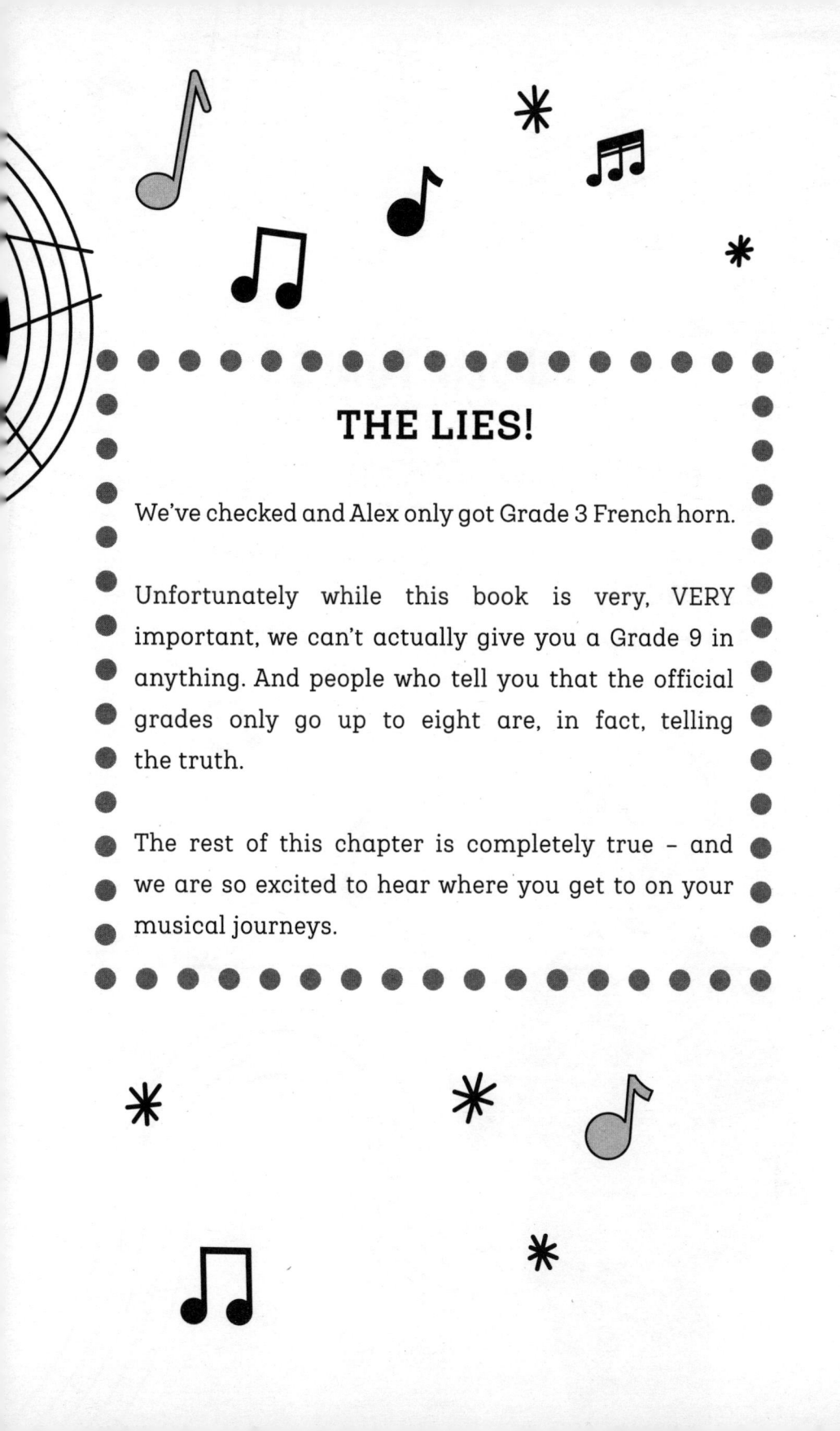

THE LIES!

We've checked and Alex only got Grade 3 French horn.

Unfortunately while this book is very, VERY important, we can't actually give you a Grade 9 in anything. And people who tell you that the official grades only go up to eight are, in fact, telling the truth.

The rest of this chapter is completely true – and we are so excited to hear where you get to on your musical journeys.

HIDDEN TUNES

OK, we lied again, there is ONE more task.

Congratulations on reading this far into the book! It's been a fun journey of facts, fibs and farting instruments. And now it is ACTUALLY time for your last task.

The band has hidden three well-known melodies within the written music that has been illustrated throughout the book. Can you spot them?

If you have an instrument, or if you can borrow one from a friend, family member or your school, use your new musical skills to work out what tunes they might be. The answers can be found on the next page!

YOUR TIME STARTS NOW.

HAPPY BIRTHDAY

Page 213

JINGLE BELLS
Page 74

THE NATIONAL ANTHEM
Page 150

ANSWERS TO RAPPER NAME QUIZ!

Here are the rappers' real names. They're not quite as cool as the ones they've invented but, for the record, we don't think there's anything wrong with being called Aubrey Graham or Cheryl James.

Cardi B is **Belcalis Almánzar**

Jay-Z is **Shawn Carter**

Drake is **Aubrey Graham**

Ludacris is **Christopher Brian Bridges**

Little Simz is **Simbiatu Abisola Abiola Ajikawo**

Queen Latifah is **Dana Elaine Owens**

50 Cent is **Curtis Jackson III**

The Notorious B.I.G. is **Christopher Wallace**

Lil Wayne is **Dwayne Carter Jr**

Missy Elliot is **Melissa Arnette Elliott**

Salt-N-Pepa is a group comprised of **Cheryl James** and **Sandra Denton**

Doja Cat is **Amala Ratna Zandile Dlamini**

Big Boi is **Antwan Patton**

MORE SONGS!

On Spotify you will find a playlist of our very own Horne Section songs, some of which are mentioned in this book.

Please follow this link to find the songs:

$$\text{https://tinyurl.com/hdzjexxt}$$

Listen, enjoy, laugh, dance, sing along, or sing something else so you can't hear it.

If you are not old enough to have a Spotify account, please ask a grown-up who has one to help you.

MORE LYRICS!

On the next few pages we've included more lyrics from two of the songs in this book, 'Dinosaur' and 'Sticky Situation'. And lyrics from a third bonus song called 'Seasons'. Enjoy!

'DINOSAUR'

I WOKE UP THIS MORNING, AND YAWNED AND STRETCHED

AND ATE UP MY TOAST AND READY BREK,

IN THE GARDEN YOU WOULD NOT BELIEVE WHAT I SAW,

A LARGE VEGETARIAN DINOSAUR,

A DIPLODOCUS NAMED ELEANOR,

AND I HAD TO ADMIT I'D NEVER SEEN HER BEFORE,

...HERBIVORE

SHE TOLD ME SHE WASN'T YET FULLY GROWN

AND SHE ALWAYS FELT LIKE SHE WAS LEFT ON HER OWN

SIX FOOT TALL, AND TWO FOOT WIDE

SHE SAID SHE JUST FELT OSTRICH SIZED

...OSTRACISED

SHE WIPED AWAY A DINOSAUR TEAR

AND I SAID ALRIGHT THEN, YOU CAN STAY HERE

I COOKED HER SOME CHIPS AND PUT ON THE TV

A SHOW ABOUT FIGHTING ON ITV

BUT JUST AS HUNTER FLEXED HIS PECKS

ALONG CAME A TYRANNOSAURUS REX

HE SWALLOWED US WHOLE WITH A SIDE OF POTATOES

AND IT WAS CLEARLY GLAD HE ATE US

... GLADIATORS

BUT THOUGH AT FIRST HE FOUND US YUMMY

THE T-REX SOON GOT A PAIN IN HIS TUMMY

THE DOCTOR SAID "WE'RE ALL OUT OF GAVISCON

AND THE RENNIES AND REMEGEL HAVE ALSO ALL GONE

BUT ANOTHER PILL HAS JUST HIT THE SHOPS

WHY DON'T YOU TRY SERATOPS,

... TRICERATOPS

'STICKY SITUATION'

SELLOTAPE, SELLOTAPE, SELLOTAPE, SELLOTAPE, SELLOTAPE, SELLOTAPE, SELLOTAPE, SELLOTAPE,

SELLOTAPE, SELLOTAPE, SELLOTAPE, SELLOTAPE, SELLOTAPE, SELLOTAPE, SELLOTAPE, SELLOTAPE,

GAFFER, GAFFER, GAFFER, GAFFER, GAFFER, GAFFER, GAFFER, GAFFER, GAFFER, GAFFER, GAFFER, GAFFER, GAFFER, GAFFER, GAFFER, GAFFER,

GAFFER, GAFFER, GAFFER, GAFFER, GAFFER, GAFFER, GAFFER, GAFFER, GAFFER, GAFFER, GAFFER, GAFFER, GAFFER, GAFFER, GAFFER, GAFFER,

MASKING TAPE, MASKING TAPE, MASKING TAPE, MASKING TAPE, MASKING TAPE,

MASKING TAPE, MASKING TAPE , MASKING TAPE, MASKING TAPE, MASKING TAPE, MASKING TAPE, MASKING TAPE, MASKING TAPE, MASKING TAPE, MASKING TAPE, MASKING TAPE,

GAFFER, GAFFER, GAFFER, GAFFER, GAFFER, GAFFER, GAFFER, GAFFER, GAFFER, GAFFER, GAFFER, GAFFER, GAFFER, GAFFER, GAFFER, GAFFER,

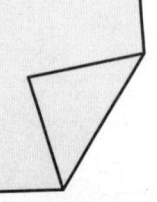

GAFFER, GAFFER, GAFFER, GAFFER, GAFFER, GAFFER, GAFFER, GAFFER, GAFFER, GAFFER, GAFFER, GAFFER, GAFFER, GAFFER, GAFFER, GAFFER,

DOUBLE-SIDED TAPE, DOUBLE-SIDED TAPE, DOUBLE-SIDED TAPE, DOUBLE-SIDED TAPE, DOUBLE-SIDED TAPE, DOUBLE-SIDED TAPE, DOUBLE-SIDED TAPE, DOUBLE-SIDED TAPE,

DOUBLE-SIDED TAPE, DOUBLE-SIDED TAPE, DOUBLE-SIDED TAPE, DOUBLE-SIDED TAPE, DOUBLE-SIDED TAPE, DOUBLE-SIDED TAPE, DOUBLE-SIDED TAPE, DOUBLE-SIDED TAPE,

GAFFER, GAFFER, GAFFER, GAFFER, GAFFER, GAFFER, GAFFER, GAFFER, GAFFER, GAFFER, GAFFER, GAFFER, GAFFER, GAFFER, GAFFER, GAFFER,

GAFFER, GAFFER, GAFFER, GAFFER, GAFFER, GAFFER, GAFFER, GAFFER, GAFFER, GAFFER, GAFFER, GAFFER, GAFFER, GAFFER, GAFFER, GAFFER.

'SEASONS'

[VERSE ONE]

WILL: WHAT'S YOUR FAVOURITE SEASON?

JOE: SPRING'S MY FAVOURITE SEASON

WILL: WHAT'S THE FLAMING REASON,
THAT SPRING'S YOUR FAVOURITE SEASON?

JOE: I LIKE TO HEAR THE ROBIN SING,
MAKES ME FEEL THE JOY WITHIN,
I LIKE TO SMELL THE CHESTNUTS ROAST,
AND ON THE FIRE, THE CRUMPETS TOAST

WILL: BUT THE ROBIN SINGS IN WINTER,
IS IT WINTER THAT YOU'RE IN TO?

JOE: YES, THEN IT MUST BE WINTER

[VERSE TWO]

WILL: WHAT'S YOUR FAVOURITE SEASON?

JOE: I RECKON WINTER'S MY FAVOURITE SEASON

WILL: WHAT'S THE RUDDY REASON
THAT WINTER'S YOUR FAVOURITE SEASON?

JOE: I LIKE THE HEAT UPON MY BACK AS I WALK DOWN
THE COUNTRY TRACK TO FEEL THE SUN UPON MY FACE
THE LONG WARM DAYS AND YOUR EMBRACE

WILL: BUT IT'S NOT HOT IN WINTER, IS IT SUMMER THAT YOU'RE IN TO'?

JOE: YES, THEN IT MUST BE SUMMER

[VERSE THREE]

WILL: WHAT'S YOUR FAVOURITE SEASON?

JOE: I'M PRETTY SURE THAT SUMMER'S MY FAVOURITE SEASON

WILL: YOU'VE SAID EVERY OTHER SEASON, DO YOU UNDERSTAND THE SEASONS?

JOE: YES. I LIKE THOSE LEAVES OF GOLDEN BROWN

WILL: NO THAT'S AUTUMN, YOU'RE A CLOWN

JOE: I LIKE THE FLOWERS WHEN IN BLOOM

WILL: NO THAT'S SPRING YOU THICK BABOON

JOE: THICK BABOON?

WILL: YOU MUST HAVE A FAVOURITE SEASON

JOE: BUT I DON'T UNDERSTAND THE SEASONS WHAT'S YOUR FAVOURITE SEASON?

WILL: MINE IS DEFINITELY FEBR-R-RUARY

GLOSSARY

album a published collection of songs that are all put together on one CD or record, or made available on a streaming service like Spotify.

amplify to make louder. Lots of musical instruments amplify a noise to make a note. For example, a saxophone amplifies the vibration of a reed and a trumpet amplifies the buzz of its player's lips. An *amplifier* is an electronic machine which increases the volume of instruments like electric guitars and microphones.

composer a person who 'writes' music, organizing sounds into a piece of music called a *composition*. This can then be performed alone or with or others – anyone can have a go, with varying degrees of success.

concerto a piece where an instrument soloist gets to show off how great they are. If (for example) the soloist plays the piano, the piece is called a *piano concerto*. Many instruments have had concertos written for them. A composer named Mike Hannickel even wrote one for the triangle.

dopamine a chemical produced in our brains that makes us feel good. If you find something fun, that will trigger the release of dopamine.

drum fill a flashy bit in a song, different to the main rhythm, which usually highlights a new section. It also often releases dopamine in the drummer, who might otherwise have become a bit bored by this point.

dynamics instructions for how loudly or quietly sections of the music should be played. It would also be a cool name for a band. In fact, there have been at least two bands called The Dynamics. It's very hard to find an original name for a band.

electrical signal a change in an electrical current which can change the pitch, tone or rhythm on an electrical instrument. There is no band called Electrical Signal. Yet.

endorphins similar to dopamine, these are chemicals produced in the brain that relieve stress and pain. There is a band from Sweden called The Endorphins.

ensemble a fancy way of saying 'group of musicians'.

genre a fancy way of saying 'style of music'.

harmony two or more different notes played and/or sung together at the same time, most often to create a pleasant sound. Nothing to do with harming one knee. (Please don't harm knees.)

improvisation 'composing' on the spot. This method of making music without preparation is most often used by jazz musicians, who can create fresh melodies on the spot, at a gig or recording session.

lyrics words set to music.

melody notes that have been organized in a pattern that is (meant to be) tuneful or enjoyable to hear.

mnemonic a pattern of letters that can be used as a prompt to remember some sort of fact or technique. 'Never Eat Shredded Wheat' is a good way of remembering the four main compass directions (North, East, South, West), unless you are the person who owns the Shredded Wheat.

molecule the smallest of all things, made up of at least two atoms bonded together (so actually not quite as small as atoms).

pitch how low or high a sound or note is. For example, a 'low' rumble of a bus driving past, or a 'high' tweet of birdsong in the morning.

rhythm the pattern of notes and sounds in a piece of music, including both the silence between and the length of each note.

shell the name for the main body of a drum. It's a hollow tube made by bending wood. Not as fragile as an egg shell and not as hard as a tortoise shell, but bigger than both, unless you're thinking of one of those enormous Galapagos tortoises.

single a published release of one song.

sonata a composition written for a solo instrument, like a violin or clarinet. It's usually written in three or four movements, or parts, and accompanied by a piano. Unless it's a *piano sonata*, which is when it's just written for the piano! Confusing, we know.

symphony a long composition to be played by a full orchestra.

tempo the speed at which a piece of music is performed. There is also a rapper called Tempo (as well as Tinie Tempah, Tina Turner and the Ting Tings).

timbre the tone and character of a musical sound. Words like 'brassy', 'reedy' or even 'warm' can be used to describe an instrument's timbre.

tone the quality of the sound that's heard

vibration when something shakes very fast; in music, this can refer to a reed on a clarinet, a string on a guitar or a cymbal on a drum kit. A musical sound is produced when the vibration is amplified through the instrument.

vocal sound created by the human voice.

voice box the simple name for the larynx, which is the part of your throat where your vocal cords produce sounds.

waveform a graphic representation of a sound wave, usually made by computer software. There are currently at least four bands called Waveform; one in the USA, one in Italy, one in the UK and one in Russia.

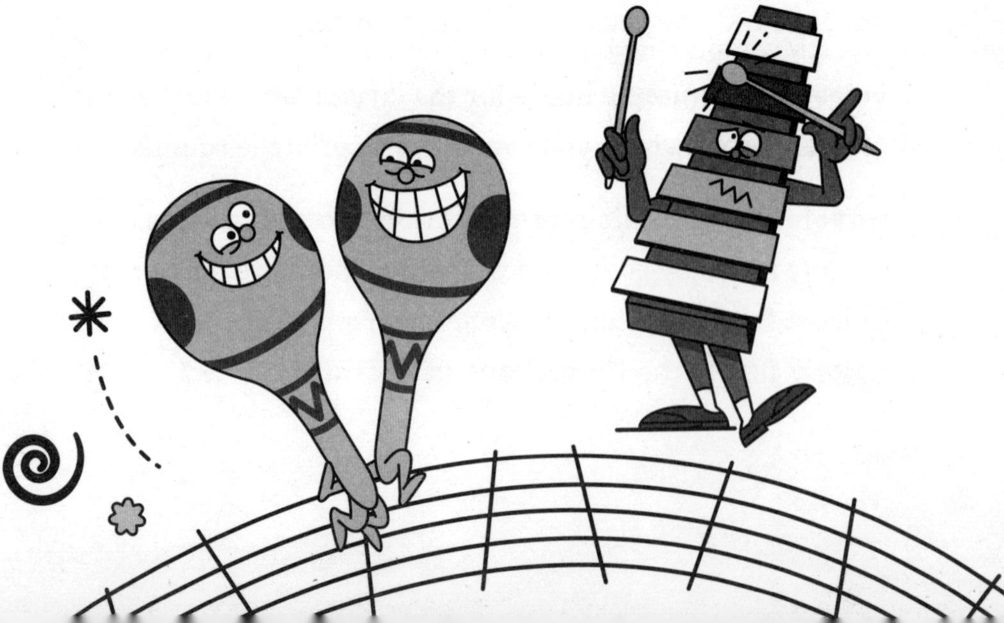

ACKNOWLEDGEMENTS

Here's to you Miss Robinson (at Midhurst Intermediate school) - you never forget a great teacher. Thanks to you and all the patient, talented, odd music teachers for everything you did for us with our music making, and all you continue to do for the musicians of the future. Thanks also to our long-suffering families for enabling us to keep the band going when there are probably more useful things we could be doing with our time and thanks too to Jonathan Taylor for his folk music expertise.

We are musicians. Well, five of us are musicians and one of us is the Taskmaster's assistant. We are not writers. Luckily some excellent people did a lot of work to make it seem like we are sort of able to write. So, finally, we'd like to thank Mary-Grace Brunker, James Taylor and everyone at Avalon, and Tom Rawlinson, Phoebe Jascourt, Emily Smyth, Pippa Shaw and everyone at Puffin for being our literary conductors. And last but certainly not least, a huge thanks to Rob Flowers for his amazing illustrations!

SONG CREDITS

The author and publisher gratefully acknowledge the permission granted to reproduce the copyright material in this book. Every effort has been made to trace copyright holders and to obtain their permission. The publisher apologises for any errors or omissions and, if notified of any corrections, will make suitable acknowledgment in future reprints or editions of this book.

Chapter One

Page 19

'I Am the Walrus' © Sony/ATV Music Publishing, 1967

Chapter Two

Page 34

For You [Album] ©Primary Wave, 1978. Published by Warner Bros

Page 47

Crazy Man Crazy [Album] © C.J.V Music, 2007. published by C.J.V Music

Chapter Three

Page 82

'Lady' © Brenda Richie Publishing/Kobalt, 1980, published by Liberty Records

Chapter Four

Page 110

Mingus Plays Piano [Album] © Impulse Records, 1964, published by Impulse!/Impulse Records

Solo Monk [Album], © Columbia Records, 1965, published by Columbia Records

Page 113

'When the Saints', © Mosaic Records, 1938, published by Decca Records

'So What' © Songs of Universal o/b/o Jazz Horn Music Corp, 1958, published by Universal

'Old McDonald', © UMG Recordings, Inc, 1966, published by Verve Records

'Birdland', © Sony Music Entertainment, Inc, 1977, published by Mulatto Music, Inc

'No Confusion' © Partisan Records, 2022

Page 129

'Hey Jude' © Sony, 1968, published by Apple.

'Purple Rain' ©Primary Wave, 1981, published by Warner Bros,

'Hit Me Baby One More Time', ©Kolbalt Music, 1998, published by Jive

'Crazy in Love' © Warner/Chappell Music Inc & Sony, 2003, published by Columbia Records and Music World entertainment

'Perfect' © Sony, 2017, published by Atlantic Records Group

'Shake It Off' (Taylor's Version) © Taylor Swift Inc, 2023, published by Republic Records

Page 132

'Cotton Fields', © Folkways Music Publishers, 1963, published by Vanguard

'Pata Pata', © Bike Music, 1967, published by Reprise

'Miyaki', © Sheffield Lab, 1985, published by Sheffield Lab

'Bold Riley', © Mechnical Copyright Protection Society Ltd, 2003 published by Pure Records

'The King of Dal Buinne', © John McSherry Music, 2016, published by Compass Records

Page 133

'Get Up, Stand Up', © Kobalt Music & Universal Music, 1973, published by Island Records

'I Shot The Sheriff', © Universal Music Corp, 1973, published by Island Records

'Three Little Birds', © Universal Music Corp, 1980, published by Tuff Gong

Page 135

'54-46 That's My Number', © Universal Music, 1968, published by Beverley's

'The Harder They Come', © Universal Music, 1972, published by Island Records

'No Woman , No Cry', © Kobalt Music, 1974, published by Island Records/Tuff Gong

'Uptown Top Ranking', © BMG Rights, 1978, published by Lightning Records

'You Don't Love Me', © BMG Rights, 1994, published by Big Beats

'Cheerleader' © Oufah Records, 2012, published by Ultra Music Publishing

Page 137

'War Pigs', ©Essex Music Int Inc, 1970, published by Vertigo Records

'Trouble Every Day', © Kolbat Music/Munchkin Music Co, 1996, published by Verve Records

'Fire', © Experience Hendrix LLC, 1970/1971, published by Track Records (UK) & Reprise Records (US)

Page 139

'Whole Lotta Love', © Warner/Chappell Music Inc, 1969, published by Atlantic Recording Corp

'Blitzkrieg Bop', © Warner/Chappell Music Inc, 1976, published by Sire Records/ABC Records

'I Love Rock 'n' Roll', © Kobalt Music, 1981, published by Boardwalk Records

'Smells like Teen Spirit', © BMG Rights/Kobalt Music, 1991 published by DGC Records

'Seven Nation Army', © Universal Music, 2003, published by XL Recordings/V2 Records

'Chaise Longue', © Domino Publishing, 2022, published by Domino Recording Company

Page 141

'Rapper's Delight', © Sony/Warner/Chappell Music Inc, 1979, published by SugarHill Records

Page 145

'Me, Myself and I', © Brigdeport Music Inc, 1989, published by Tommy Boys Records

'Jump', © EMI Music, 1992, published by Ruffhouse Records

'Kid's Rapper's Delight Kids Rap-Along', © Warner/Chappell Music Inc, 1999, published by Rhino Entertainment

'I Wish', © Red Brick Songs, 1986, published by Scotti Brothers Records

'Killing Me Softly', © Warner/Chappell Music Inc, 1996, published by Capital Records

Chapter Five

Page 154

'Meet the Flintstones', © Warner/Chappell Music Inc, 1963, published by Warner-Tamerlane Pub Corp

'Sweet Caroline', © Universal Music, 1969, published Uni Records/MCA Records

Page 164

'Good Day Sunshine', © Sony/Kobalt Music, 1966, published by Parlophone Records Ltd

'Space Oddity', © Essex Music Int Inc, 1969, published by Phillips Records (UK) & Mercury Records (US)

Page 165

'Under The Sea', © Walt Disney Records, 1988, published by Walt Disney Records

Page 214

'Birthday', © Sony, 1968, published by Apple Records

'Fingertips', © Universal Music, 1963, published by Tamla

Page 215

'All I Want For Christmas Is You', © Universal Music, 1994, published by Columbia Records

Page 224

'The People's Army', © Tunecore Digital Music, 2001, published by Dogday Records

Chapter Eight

Page 237

'White Christmas,' © Universal Music, 1942, published by Decca Records/MCA Records

Page 241

'Ding Ding Song' © The Horne Section 2023

Page 245

'We Will Rock You', © EMI Music, 1977, published by EMI (UK) & Elektra (US)

'Single Ladies', © Warner/Chappell Music Inc, 2008, published by Columbia Records

'Happy', © EMI Music, 2013, published by Columbia Records

Page 246

The Lion King (Original Motion Picture Soundtrack) © Walt Disney Records, 1994, published by Walt Disney Records

Page 247

Joseph and the Amazing Technicolor Dream Coat (Album), © Universal Music, 1973, published by RSO Records

Jesus Christ Superstar [Album], © Universal, 1970, published by Decca Records/MCA

Yesterday, © Sony, 1965, published by Capitol Records (US) & Parlophone Records UK

Page 248

'Oops! . . . I Did It Again', © Kobalt Music Publishing, 2000, published by Jive Records

Page 250 & 251

'Thick and Creamy', 'Sticky Situation' & 'Chris Hoy' © The Horne Section 2023

Page 253

'Being with you' © The Horne Section 2023

Page 254

'Dinosaur' © The Horne Section 2023

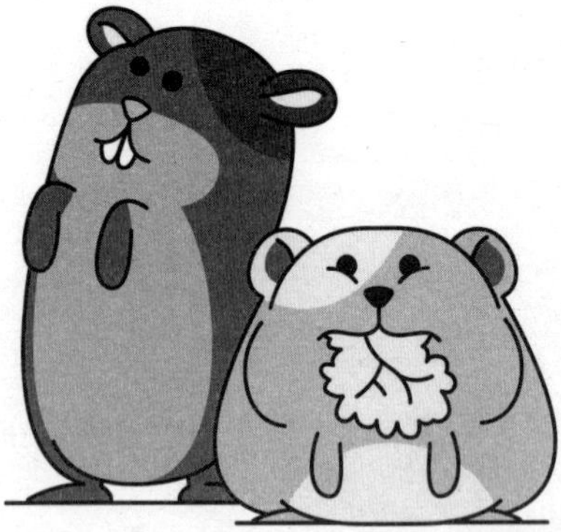